"A terrific book, a confident, honest, personal, and lively effort."

—*The Oregonian*

"*Embedded Balls* is filled with funny stuff and great observations about our world. If I steal some of the lines from this book to use as a commentator, do I have to give credit?" —Paul Azinger

"Peter has always made me laugh, and he'll make you laugh, too. He did it with *Buried Lies* and he's done it again with *Embedded Balls*. A great inside look at the world of professional golf." —Fred Couples

"Peter understands as well as anyone the life of the touring pro—the ups and downs, the highs and lows—what makes us tick. It's all here in *Embedded Balls*." —John Daly

"Peter thinks he's a rock 'n' roll musician and I think I'm a golfer. Talk about self-delusion! But man, is he funny." —Huey Lewis

"I've learned a lot from Peter through the years. I learned a lot more from this book! This is required reading for all true golfers."

—Chris DiMarco

Praise for
Buried Lies

"Pleasant and amiable." —*Publishers Weekly*

"Opinionated, insightful, and provocative." —*Library Journal*

"Delightful . . . An entertaining look at pro golf's lighter side."

—*Kirkus Reviews*

Also by Peter Jacobsen

Buried Lies

EMBEDDED

BALLS

Adventures on and off the Tour with Golf's Premier Storyteller

PETER JACOBSEN

with

JACK SHEEHAN

BERKLEY BOOKS, NEW YORK

THE BERKLEY PUBLISHING GROUP
Published by the Penguin Group
Penguin Group (USA) Inc.
375 Hudson Street, New York, New York 10014, USA
Penguin Group (Canada), 90 Eglinton Avenue East, Suite 700, Toronto, Ontario M4P 2Y3, Canada
(a division of Pearson Penguin Canada Inc.)
Penguin Books Ltd., 80 Strand, London WC2R 0RL, England
Penguin Group Ireland, 25 St. Stephen's Green, Dublin 2, Ireland (a division of Penguin Books Ltd.)
Penguin Group (Australia), 250 Camberwell Road, Camberwell, Victoria 3124, Australia
(a division of Pearson Australia Group Pty. Ltd.)
Penguin Books India Pvt. Ltd., 11 Community Centre, Panchsheel Park, New Delhi—110 017, India
Penguin Group (NZ), Cnr. Airborne and Rosedale Roads, Albany, Auckland 1310, New Zealand
(a division of Pearson New Zealand Ltd.)
Penguin Books (South Africa) (Pty.) Ltd., 24 Sturdee Avenue, Rosebank, Johannesburg 2196, South Africa

Penguin Books Ltd., Registered Offices: 80 Strand, London WC2R 0RL, England

While the author has made every effort to provide accurate telephone numbers and Internet addresses at
the time of publication, neither the publisher nor the author assumes any responsibility for errors, or for
changes that occur after publication. Further, the publisher does not have any control over and does not
assume any responsibility for author or third-party websites or their content.

PRINTING HISTORY
G. P. Putnam's Sons hardcover edition / October 2005
Berkley trade paperback edition / October 2006

Berkely trade paperback ISBN: 0-425-21178-9

Library of Congress has catalogued the G. P. Putnam's Sons hardcover edition of this book as follows:

Jacobsen, Peter, 1954–
Embedded balls : adventures on and off the Tour with golf's premier storyteller / Peter Jacobsen with
Jack Sheehan.
p.   cm.
ISBN 0-399-15316-0
1. Golf—Anecdotes.   2. Golf—Tournaments—Anecdotes.   3. Golf—Humor.   4. Jacobsen, Peter,
1954–   I. Sheehan, Jack.
GV967.J23   2005
796.352—dc22   2005051183

PRINTED IN THE UNITED STATES OF AMERICA

10   9   8   7   6   5   4   3   2   1

To my mother, Barbara Jacobsen Gustavson, who always showed me love and support. There was a time when she was the only one who thought my golf impressions were worth watching. I practiced them just for her. And to Jan, Amy, Kristen, and Mick, who've been with me every step of the way. And to my brother David and sister, Susan, whose laughter always brightens my day.

CONTENTS

Introduction   *1*

1 • Memories of Payne   9

2 • Tinseltown and Big John   25

3 • Plugged In   *41*

4 • A Breakout Year   *55*

5 • Hartford in My Heart   *73*

6 • Please . . . I'm Trying to Concentrate Here   *83*

7 • A Senior Moment . . . Interrupted   *91*

8 • The U.S. Senior Open: How It All Went Down   *107*

9 • The Pros and the Ams   *131*

10 • Tiger and Fluff . . . and Other Stuff   *147*

11 • Carrying On a "Tradition"   *163*

12 • Things We Can Do Better   *183*

Acknowledgments   *207*

EMBEDDED BALLS

Introduction

I CAN'T BELIEVE it's been twelve years since Jack Sheehan and I wrote *Buried Lies: True Tales and Tall Stories from the PGA Tour.* Back then I was considered an old fart on the flat-belly tour, and now I'm a young punk on the fat-belly tour. But I still tee it up on the younger circuit several weeks a year just to test myself and because I'm not ready to quit playing some of my favorite courses and hanging out with some of my favorite people. As I've said in interviews, I may not be as good a player as I once was, but I have the capability to be as good for one week as I ever was. I proved that to myself and the doubting public when I won the Greater Hartford Open two years ago at the age of forty-nine. I hadn't won in eight years and I know some people think I must have cut over on about the 15th hole to shoot the scores I did and beat those youngsters, but I promise I didn't cheat. You can look it up. The whole damn thing was on television.

Two of my favorite people, Payne Stewart and Jack Lemmon, are no longer with us, and I miss them both terribly. The former was my partner in a garage band, Jake Trout and the Flounders, and the other was my partner in crime—the crime of missing about eighteen consecutive cuts in the AT&T National Pro-Am at Pebble Beach. As I said in my eulogy at Jack's funeral, I can never tee it up at Pebble again without seeing Lemmon hit his patented big-ass slice off the first tee and yelling so loudly that everyone lined up along both sides of the fairway and in downtown Carmel could hear, "There goes a PIECE-A-SHIIIIIIIT!"

One time Lem actually hit a duck slice off that tee that bounced off a tree, went through the open door of the lodge, and into a bathroom. "I hope they flush that sucker down the toilet, where it belongs," he said.

I share some other Lemmon moments, and memories of Payne, in the following pages.

Another great man I lost just about the time the first book was going to print was my father, Erling Jacobsen, whom everyone called Jake. Dad fought throat and colon cancer and other ailments bravely before we lost him in the summer of 1992. My father was a gentleman golfer, a wonderfully kind and intelligent man, and a success in his insurance business. But what he knew about popular culture or the stuff you'd read in *People* magazine you could put in a thimble. He was all about his work and his family and the game of golf. Anyway, shortly after my parents divorced, in the early 1980s, I decided to take my dad to Vail, Colorado, for a short vacation. Dad had been spending a lot of time at home, and he was really struggling with being single again. He didn't have a clue how to keep a house or prepare a meal. He would have needed a cookbook to boil water.

The occasion of the trip was the Gerald Ford Invitational, a pro-celebrity event that raised a lot of money for charity. I had been on the Tour just five years, had one victory under my belt, and was not what you'd call a "name" player in the field. So I was surprised when I saw my pairing for the first round. I was scheduled to play with none other than Clint Eastwood. I remember thinking how cool it would be for my dad to watch me play with an American icon, but I wanted him to be surprised when he showed up at the course the next day, so I didn't say anything. Dad was already on cloud nine because after we'd flown in to Vail, we were joined on the bus ride to the hotel by Joe Garagiola, who back then was the color commentator on baseball's game of the week. Baseball being one of the few things my dad watched on television, he thought it was the coolest thing ever that he had made a buddy out of a major celebrity like Joe. We could have ended the trip right there with the bus ride and Dad would have thought it was a great vacation. I couldn't help thinking he'd be bowled over when he met the number-one box-office star in the world the next day.

We had begun the round and were walking down the fairway, and I asked my playing partners if they minded if my dad walked with us between the ropes, because the gallery was very large. Of course all the people were there to see Clint. And on about the 4th hole, we had a little holdup, so Dad walked over to Eastwood and said, "So Clint, what do you do?"

And Clint kind of smiled and looked at my dad and realized that he was serious, that he had no idea who he was. And that really tickled him. He also probably felt sorry for my dad, thinking, Where the hell has this son of a bitch been that he doesn't know who I am? But he was very polite and said, "I'm an actor."

I was dying of embarrassment at this exchange, and couldn't believe my dad had done this, but what could I do?

So Dad said, "Oh, the hell you are. Have you been in anything I might know?"

And Clint said, "Well, let's see. I've done the *Dirty Harry* movies and *The Good, the Bad, and the Ugly,* and a few others."

And Dad said, "Nope . . . no . . . I haven't seen any of those."

So Clint mentioned a couple others, but those drew a blank as well.

And finally it got down to where Eastwood mentioned that one of his first roles was in a television series called *Rawhide,* and my dad lit up.

"Oh, yeah. You were Rowdy Yates. I loved that show."

And from that point on Dad called him Rowdy, and they got along famously.

SINCE THE FIRST BOOK WAS PUBLISHED, I have done a lot of stuff. I spent a year as a golf commentator for ABC Sports, won back-to-back tournaments, and led the money list for half a season. Along with my partner Jim Hardy, I've designed about a dozen golf courses, put my name on a game called Golden Tee that has created a cult following of bar rats I'm proud to call my own, produced a couple of ongoing shows on the Golf Channel that endeavor to take some of the stiffness out of the game, watched Peter Jacobsen Productions grow into one of the most respected event management firms in the country, and seen Jan's and my three children grow into fine young adults. It's been a good ride.

I like to think that some of these accomplishments may one day overshadow my previous career high point, which was to be the only PGA Tour player in history to make an unassisted tackle in a major championship. For those who don't remember, that happened in the Open Championship at Royal St. George's in 1985. Please forgive me if you know the story, but it bears repeating:

I was in the third to last group on the final day, playing with Tom Kite. Right behind us was Sandy Lyle, who would win the tournament. I was preparing to pitch onto the 18th green when the most astonishing thing happened. One of the marshals posted behind the green ripped off his slicker and started running around the green, naked as a jaybird. It was so stunning it took me a minute to comprehend that it was really happening. I just watched in amazement. The dude was pretty quick, and before anyone made a move to interrupt his chicken dance, he was making a second lap, then a third, this time directly at Kite, who made a nifty matador move to avoid contact.

The gallery was laughing loudly by this time, and I learned later that the ABC and BBC cameras had long before shifted the cameras away from him. This was way beyond what we now call a "wardrobe malfunction." This was a scrawny idiot showing the world what little he had to offer. About this time—we'll call it lap four of his mile run—the bobbies that were there for security reasons took up the chase. They were charging toward us with their nightsticks and whistles and those great hats with the chinstraps. Meanwhile, the streaker was coming directly at me, and he was leaving his bony footprints right in the line of my chip shot. It also occurred to me as I was watching this farce unfold that Sandy Lyle was waiting in the fairway, trying to win his first major championship, and that this was an unparalleled distraction that could cost him the title. As the guy came closer to me, I got down in my best Ray Lewis stance and put a couple head-jukes on him to let him know I was ready for business. I remembered from playing tackle football as a kid that you don't want to look at a runner's head or eyes; you need to aim for his midsection. So when the guy got about 5 feet from me, I lowered my shoulder and dove at his hips. I made certain I turned my head at the last minute so I wouldn't end up with a mouth full of parsley.

I could hear the wind rush out of his lungs as I drove him to the ground. Just then the bobbies dog-piled him and for a quick moment it looked like I could have started a hell of an orgy, but instead they pulled him up off the ground and led him from the green. As long as play was being held up anyway, I did a little sack dance to commemorate the event, and then I held up my thumb and index finger an inch apart to let the fans know that this guy was literally no big deal. Sure enough, the next day the picture of my intimate moment made the front page of the London *Times,* while poor Sandy Lyle's victory in the Open had to take second billing.

I've been asked many times whether I know what happened to the only naked man I've ever embraced. I really don't know. Other than the occasional love sonnet and bouquet he sends on special occasions, I'm not sure what he's up to.

WE TOLD OTHER FUN STORIES in *Buried Lies,* like the time Raymond Floyd's bleary-eyed caddie Adolphus Hull, nicknamed Golf Ball, was feeling the effects of a long night in the 19th hole. Early the next morning, just before the first round was to tee off, Golf Ball grabbed the yardage book from the wrong Colonial Country Club (the one in Fort Worth rather than in Memphis), and because he kept giving Raymundo yardages from the wrong course, forced Floyd to get it up and down five times in a row from 20 yards over the green.

And we shared the incident at Cypress Point when Greg Norman and Clint Eastwood pelted golf balls at a Porta Potti they thought featured Jack Lemmon on the throne, only to have an eighty-year-old woman peek her head out the plastic door after a long spell and inquire whether it was "safe to come out now." I'm certain that woman needed counseling before she ever used outdoor plumbing again.

We also told the story of my younger brother Paul, who died of AIDS in the late summer of 1988. No chapter in the book, which was for the most part as light and airy as a helium balloon, touched more people than that one. Jack Sheehan and I went back and forth for weeks about whether or not we should include Paul's story in the book. Jack thought it was important to include, to dramatize how a touring pro's life is not all wine and roses. He also liked the biblical symbolism of two brothers named Peter and Paul following such different paths in life. My family, on the other hand, was concerned about the appropriateness of sharing such a personal story when it had not even been openly discussed among ourselves.

We ultimately decided to go with Paul's story, which we titled "A Candle in the Wind," and no single chapter generated nearly as much positive feedback. Virtually every reviewer said the "Paul chapter" was the most memorable in the book. And I should say that telling that story provided solace and closure for our family. Shortly after the book's release, I received a letter from Elton John, one of my musical heroes, and he thanked me for contributing to AIDS awareness. The chapter was even included in a collection of stories, *Chicken Soup for the Golfer's Soul,* which was the best-selling sports book in the world in 1999.

AFTER *BURIED LIES* WAS RELEASED, Sheehan and I felt that we had at least one more book in us, and so my turning fifty and joining the Champions Tour in March 2004 gave us just the excuse we needed to launch a mulligan. Little did we know that just five weeks after my Champions debut in Valencia, California, where I finished third, my hip would require surgery and I would be shelved from competition for ten weeks. Of course, all the indignities of surgery and painkillers and revealing hospital gowns gave us fodder for an entire chapter on humiliation and self-deprecation. As we were trying to re-create those wonderful moments in the hospital, I told Jack that had I been a coyote I would have chewed my own leg off at the hip. It hurt ten times worse than a four-putt from 3 feet with my Tour card on the line.

But what d'ya know? A fraction over three months after I was lying crippled in a hospital bed, I managed to go out and win the biggest tournament in the world for guys half a century old, the United States Senior Open. I even amazed myself with that one. But I'd be remiss if I didn't give a big tip of the visor to my wife, Jan, and to Dr. Marc Phillipon: she, for her unwavering support, and he, for his medical expertise and skill, which allowed me to recover quickly and get back to chasing that fickle little spheroid. The fact that I had to play thirty-six holes in brutal heat the last day of the Senior Open is further testament to what a great job Dr. Phillipon did fixing my broken body.

We'll go into greater detail on all these stories in the following pages, and a whole lot more: how John Daly almost decapitated a spectator; what players *really* say to each other in the locker room; why getting on *Sportscenter* is not always a good thing; how Payne Stewart got back at Paul Azinger for beating him in a tournament (moral: always check your shoes before putting them on); why loaning Tiger Woods your caddie can be a mistake; what made Arnold Palmer change his shorts; and how I won the U.S. Open by outdueling Kevin Costner and Don Johnson down the stretch.

With *Embedded Balls* we hope to bring along a new audience of golfers to accompany our friends who read the first book. So why not join us? Grab your sticks, change your shoes, and let's go another round.

—Peter Jacobsen

1

Memories of Payne

I DIDN'T BECOME FRIENDS with Payne Stewart right away. I'd been on Tour four or five years when he came out, and it was obvious to all of us right away that Payne had a lot of game. He'd won a couple of Asian Tour events and one in Australia, and in his first full year on the PGA Tour he won at Quad Cities. I guess the best way to say it was that from the time he got his card, Payne was very, very confident in his ability, and he wasn't a guy I warmed to immediately.

He wore long pants the first couple years on Tour, and looked just like everybody else. I think he was frustrated that no one really recognized or acknowledged him, because he knew in his heart he was a special player. He got the idea to wear knickers from Stewart Ginn, an international player who now competes with me on the Champions Tour. I remember Payne told some of us he was thinking of going with the knickers, and I thought that was pretty bold. You'd see them on marshals sometimes, and a few Senior Tour guys wore them. I remember Billy Casper wearing plus fours in red, white, and blue. Coming down the fairway, he looked like a walking post office. But that's the fashion statement that Payne chose because he wanted to set himself apart.

Then when he signed a big contract with the National Football League to wear team colors from week to week, he really started to have fun with it and became known as a personality with a great sense of style. I have to admit, he looked pretty snazzy with those gold-toed shoes and white knicker socks and Ben Hogan–style cap, and there was no denying that a guy had to be pretty secure in his masculinity to pull off that look.

Through the years, Payne just got better as a player and a person. Because of the combination of his talent and fashion flair, he was certainly one of the most recognizable players in the game in the 1990s, maybe even *the* most recognizable.

Payne was a great practical joker and loved to stick it in your face. He would be playing in Dallas and he'd wear the Washington Redskins' colors on Saturday, just to goad the fans. Some of them would taunt him, but he'd just laugh and feed off the energy. It raised his level of determination to play well, and I think it helped him play better. But then he'd come back on Sunday wearing the Cowboys' colors, and the fans would be right back cheering for him. He had that little boy smile and wink in his eye so that people always knew he was just messing with them.

I remember how he "punked" my caddie Mike "Fluff" Cowan one year down in New Orleans. We were on the range warming up for a Tuesday practice round, and Payne walked up with his cap sorta pulled down low over his eyes. Payne's longtime caddie Mike Hicks was with him. And Payne mumbled, "Hey, guys, what's up?" He was holding his hand over his mouth.

And Fluff said, "Payne, you got a toothache or something?"

"Ah, man," he said. "It's worse than that. I was down in the French Quarter last night and had a couple drinks and this guy comes up and tries to take my wallet. I pushed him back and he popped me in the mouth."

At that point Payne removed his hand and showed Mike his teeth. Two of them were broken off and another looked like it was wedged up under his gum line. And there was a big old gap in the middle, sort of like David Letterman's, only wider. His mouth resembled the backwoods guy in the movie *Deliverance* who terrorized poor Ned Beatty and Burt Reynolds. It looked totally real, and totally messed up.

Fluff said, "Oh my God, Payne. You can't play like that. You need to see an orthodontist and get something figured out."

Payne played it perfectly straight and said, "Ah, man. I can play, but it hurts like a mother."

I noticed that Hicksie had turned around and his shoulders were shaking, because he knew Payne had set the hook deep in Fluff's lip and was reeling him in like a trophy sailfish. And just then Payne popped the set of fangs out. They were a novelty-shop gag called Billy-Bob Teeth. Payne just stared at Fluff like he was the biggest sucker in North America. And Fluff dropped my golf bag and took off and chased him all the way down to the end of the range. Payne liked his little prank so much that he pulled it on about five other guys before the week was out.

In hindsight, Fluff could have gotten the ultimate touché, because he doesn't have *any* real teeth. His choppers had all been Yankee-doodled. When he would stay at our house, he'd sometimes pop the dentures and put the mugwump face on my kids. To them it was like seeing Jason from *Friday the 13th,* in a jumpsuit.

WHEN I THINK OF PAYNE, I also think of 1989, when he won the PGA at Kemper Lakes outside Chicago. It was his first major, and he won it in an unusual way. He made a great back-nine charge, birdieing four of the last six holes for a final-round 67, but when he signed his scorecard he was still two strokes behind Mike Reid on the leader board. But Mike had problems getting it to the house, and when he bogeyed three of the last five holes, the tournament belonged to Payne.

I had finished my final round earlier and was back at the hotel packing to leave as Reid was bogeying the final hole. I decided to drive back to the course to be there with Payne and celebrate his win. When I got there, he was super pumped up. I arrived in time for the private celebration with the bigwigs from the PGA, Pat Reilly and Jim Awtrey and other dignitaries. When I congratulated Payne, he gave me a huge bear hug and damn near crushed my ribs. Payne had thrown down a couple glasses of champagne to celebrate, and when he went to the john I followed him in there. He was so excited about winning a major that he was actually running and planting a foot on the bathroom wall and trying to run up it. He was acting like he'd holed a full wedge shot on the last hole to win, when in reality he had sat there watching a fellow professional who was a friend of ours crash and burn, something that happens to every player at one time or another. I was concerned with what might happen in the ceremony to follow, and in subsequent conversations with the media. So I actually grabbed him by the shoulders, the same way I would do with my son Mick when he was acting up as a kid, and I held him against the wall.

I said, "Payne, stop and shut up for a minute! You just won the PGA Championship. That's huge. And I'm ecstatic for you. That's why I came back to celebrate. But you have to gather yourself. While you're jumping up the wall, a friend of ours is probably dying inside from having blown the tournament. When you go out there, you can't be butt-slapping and doing high fives. You have to talk about how your friend Mike Reid played great, and how he would have made a great PGA champion as well. You need to show some respect for him, and stop being a jerk."

It's one of those things I never would have done if I hadn't considered Payne such a good friend. And Payne understood what I was saying, and he went back and praised Mike Reid and did all the right things. Oh, I'm sure there was a part of him that was probably upset with me for pissing on his parade, but two weeks later, when I next saw him at a tournament, he came over and thanked me for helping him get his act together that day. I think that moment really cemented our friendship.

THEN THERE WAS THE MEMORIAL TOURNAMENT at Muirfield Village in 1993, the year that Payne's good friend Paul Azinger dunked a bunker shot on the final hole and stole the tournament from him. I was doing the television broadcast for ABC that year and was upstairs with Payne in the locker room shortly after we went off the air, packing to leave. As Zinger was giving interviews in the press room, I watched Payne cut up a bunch of old bananas and stuff them into the toes of Paul's dress shoes. I then sat down with Payne and had a beer, just the two of us. Obviously, he was tremendously disappointed. Payne had held a one-shot lead going to the final hole, and was standing in the fairway on 18 when Zinger holed that bunker shot and dropped to his knees and raised his arms. The shot is on nearly every golf highlight reel you'll ever see. Meantime, Payne's ball is sitting smack dab in the middle of a sand-filled divot in the fairway. He'd pulled his second shot into the same bunker Paul had been in five minutes before and failed to get it up and down. It was the kind of bitter loss that can take months to shake off, but instead Payne the practical joker decided to get a small measure of revenge.

About twenty minutes later, Zinger came up the stairs from the press room, and we chatted briefly. He and Payne were actually traveling together that week. Then we watched him start to slip on his shoes, and he got that look on his face that people get when they've just encountered something soft and squishy.

"What the . . ." he shouted, as banana goo dripped off his fingers.

"I just had to pay you back for that shot on eighteen," Payne said.

It makes me laugh even today.

I WILL NEVER FORGET when we recorded the first cassette of Jake Trout and the Flounders in Tallahassee. We did it in a studio owned by Butch Trucks, who played drums for the Allman Brothers Band. Most of the background music had been done, I had already sung a lot of the vocals, and Mark Lye had contributed some serious guitar work. All we needed was for Payne to fly up from Orlando to put some sweet harmonica behind our work. I picked Payne up at the Tallahassee airport, and as we were driving to the studio he started getting nervous. He said, "What the hell are we doing here?"

And I said, "We're recording an album."

"We have no business recording an album," he said. "We suck."

"Of course we suck," I said. "But we've got nothing to lose. If *Rolling Stone* pans us, do we care? We're supposed to suck."

"But I double suck on the harmonica," Payne said.

I told him it was too late, that he was committed to the project and that we'd already paid for the studio time, and that even though he sucked on the mouth organ he needed to get it together and play his ass off. The truth is, he was pretty good. Payne was no better or worse on the harmonica than Mark was on the guitar, or I was on the vocals. In musical terms, we were all 12-handicappers, but we were having a blast, and what we were doing in this professional setting was not much different from a weekend amateur golfer teeing it up in a Tour pro-am.

So we arrived at the recording studio and got Payne all hooked up and in the soundproof booth. It's a neat process. You've got your soundboard, you get your headphones on, and then they run the music and the vocals and you lay down your tracks.

But there's a pressure involved in making a recording that is much greater than performing live. When Jake Trout and the Flounders did concerts, we were backed by great musicians like Steve Cropper and Donald "Duck" Dunn, who had performed with Booker T. and the MGs and with the Blues Brothers. As golfers we would get up there with them and feed off the energy and the great music. We'd do our thing and laugh at one another and the audience would really get into it and everyone would have a great time. But working in a recording studio is a different deal. It's much quieter and you feel a far greater pressure to perform well.

Once Payne was in the booth and starting to lay his tracks down, I could tell he was not comfortable. He clearly wasn't feeling the groove, and the music just wasn't happening. Duck was in the studio helping to produce, and he, too, could see it wasn't happening. After about two hours, we hadn't come up with anything we could use.

So Payne took off the headphones and grabbed my arm and said, "C'mon. We need to take a drive."

Even though it was only eleven in the morning, we drove to a convenience store and bought a six-pack. On the way back to the studio, Payne tossed down about five beers. To keep up the camaraderie, and because I'd already finished my vocals, I drank the other one. We got back to the studio and Duck Dunn and I started talking Payne through the process, and we could see that the beer had taken the edge off and he was now floating slowly into never-never land. He put on his jet-black shades, turned off all the lights, retreated into the recording booth, and leaned his chair back against the wall. And he laid down the prettiest, most mellow harmonica tracks you've ever heard. Once those five tall boys had adjusted his attitude, the problem was solved.

I got Payne to the airport to catch his flight with about five minutes to spare, and I called his wife, Tracey, and told her that Payne had drunk a little too much lunch, and that she needed to guide him off the plane when he landed. The irony of that day is that here was a guy who could stay as calm as a summer pond in Georgia with the pressure of major championships on the line, but when it came to playing a little mouth organ in a recording studio he choked like a chicken. Go figure that.

In 1995, I fell into a nice rhythm where the fairways looked a mile wide and the cup looked like a bucket. In early February, I won my favorite tournament, the AT&T Pebble Beach National Pro-Am, by shooting 17 under par with a Sunday 65 that has to rank as one of my best-ever rounds under pressure. And the momentum carried over to the next week, when I won the Buick Invitational of California at Torrey Pines. Golf is such a funny game, you never know when the stars will fall into perfect alignment for you, but it sure is fun when you get on that kind of a roll. Naturally, the press was assuming I would go for three victories in a row the following week. The Bob Hope Chrysler Classic was next on the schedule, and everyone knew that it was one of my favorite events. I had eked out a narrow victory there in 1990, birdieing the last hole to win by a stroke. I talked about the importance of that victory in *Buried Lies,* and how on the last couple of holes I was fighting off the emotion of losing my brother Paul to AIDS two years before, and how he had been treated for drug dependency near the golf course at the Betty Ford Center.

The reason I was skipping the Hope for the first time in many years was that my wife, Jan, was turning forty, and I was going to throw a little party for her. Jan knew that we were going to do something for her birthday, but she had no idea that for months I had been planning a surprise party that she'd never forget—one that would include about four hundred of her closest friends, and include a surprise ending that would blow everybody away.

I rented a local dance hall, catered in the food, and hired two bands to play. One singer was a Rod Stewart impersonator named Rob Hanna, who had headlined in Las Vegas and Reno; he came out first and did a killer one-hour Stewart tribute. A good friend of ours named Jean Humphrey came out of the ladies' room, turned the corner, saw Rob Hanna onstage, heard him singing, and screamed, "Oh my God, Peter has hired Rod Stewart!" It took her about two songs to realize that Rob Hanna wasn't the real deal. Then I got onstage, took the mike, and said, "I hope you enjoyed our opening act. And now I want to introduce a terrific young band from San Francisco. You probably haven't heard of them but you will soon. Please welcome Herbie Levine and the Jews!"

Everybody gave a great ovation, and the curtain rose, and their first song started. It was "The Power of Love." And I remember watching the expressions of the people up front. Their faces absolutely dropped when they realized who was actually playing: it was Huey Lewis and the News.

I was proud of the fact that I had been able to keep the secret, with the help of the great staff at Peter Jacobsen Productions, and that none of the guests or Jan had had a clue I was bringing in one of the best rock bands in the world. And Huey and the guys didn't even charge me. All they asked for was a set of new golf clubs each.

But the point of the story as it relates to Payne Stewart is the effort he put into doing something special for Jan that night. I had asked several of our close friends in the golf and entertainment worlds to put together video messages for Jan. I then turned the tape over to an editor to put together something she could keep and treasure forever. We got videos back from Jack Nicklaus, Arnold Palmer, Jack Lemmon, Bruce Hornsby, Ray Floyd, Huey Lewis, Ben Crenshaw, and many more. These guys are such pros at doing stuff like that, that they were able to knock their bits out in about five or ten minutes. Payne was the only one of all the people I asked who worried about it for weeks, asked me several questions about what exactly he should do, and then practiced it for a long time before actually putting his message on video. In it, he did an amazing impersonation of Forrest Gump, which won the Oscar for best movie that year. It was about that time that a lot of people were going around saying, "Life is like a box of chocolates..." in a slow, halting voice. But Payne had the cadence down pat.

So I got this raw footage videotape from Payne, and on it he does this impersonation and the voice and cadence are perfect. And Tracey was sitting with him. And he starts out with: "Hi, Jan... This is Forrest... Forrest Gump... Here with Tracey... And we just want to say happy birthday... to you... You are a friend... a friend of ours... and a good friend... You are pretty... And you are forty...."

It was hilarious, but in the raw footage that he sent me, you could see that it took Payne about four tries to do it without breaking up. He had the voice down so well that either he or Tracey would start laughing and ruin the take. It was kind of like the session with the harmonica on our first Jake Trout CD. If Payne was going to do something, he was going to get it right or bust his butt trying.

PAYNE WAS SO GREAT WITH PEOPLE, especially golf fans. He loved to interact with them, which is one of the reasons we became such close friends. Like him, I've never met a conversation I didn't want to join in on.

When we did our CD, *I Love to Play,* Payne and Mark Lye and I filmed a music video for VH1 in Culver City outside Los Angeles. We were driving up and down a side street in a goofy-looking golf cart, hamming it up over the music, when a Japanese gas station owner suddenly recognized Payne and came running out, screaming his name. The guy was going crazy. He was obviously totally frenzied over spotting Payne, and then suddenly the guy's wife appeared and showed us a photo of the two of them with Payne, from a pro-am golf tournament years before in Japan. And the next thing you know out came Grandma and the kids and the neighbors.

Payne was just as engaging as could be with these people. He chatted with them for about twenty minutes as our camera crew got set to do another take, and he posed for pictures, and none of it was forced. I could tell he was really enjoying himself and appreciated being recognized and made a big deal over. I can think of so many other superstars in sports who would have run from a scene like that, and would not have wanted to be bothered, but the courtesy he showed them all I'm sure was something that family talks about even to this day.

But that was typical of Payne. He was more patient with fans than the average player. He didn't get throngs like Tiger Woods does today, but there was always a crowd of people around him, to either get an autograph or hear a story. I would often see him after a round sitting on some stairs with a bottle of water, with fans just talking to him as he signed hats and programs or told stories.

The way Payne died was so eerie and so memorable, especially since it was at the very height of his career and his glory. It was almost like James Dean's sudden death when he was on his way to being crowned the new king of Hollywood, or Marilyn Monroe, dying at age thirty-six in the prime of her career. At the time of his death, Payne was the reigning U.S. Open champion and a vital member of the victorious American Ryder Cup team, which just one month before had beaten the Europeans so dramatically at Brookline with a great Sunday comeback.

Who can ever forget the way he made that incredible 15-footer at Pinehurst to nip Phil Mickelson for his second U.S. Open crown? And the way he punched his fist in the air and lifted Mike Hicks off the ground brought tears to every golfer's eyes. It has become an indelible image in American sport. And the way he graciously put his hands on Phil's face, and had the presence of mind to try to ease Phil's pain at losing by saying to him, with Phil's wife, Amy, expecting their first child any hour, "You are going to be a father. That is the greatest thing that can happen in your life. You are so lucky." Wow, it chokes me up even now thinking about it.

On October 25, 1999, I was on the treadmill at home in Portland, working out, when Jan came in and said, "Turn it to CNN. They've lost contact with a plane. It's a chartered flight, and it's a professional golfer, and they cannot contact the plane."

I immediately thought of Arnold Palmer, and got a sick feeling in my stomach. I got off the treadmill and sat on the couch. It was about eleven A.M., and Jan and I watched all the reports. A plane had taken off from Orlando at nine-twenty, with two crew and three passengers aboard. Everything was fine, but then a few minutes in, the tower couldn't reach the pilots anymore—there was nothing, just dead silence. Military fighter jets scrambled up to peer inside, but the cockpit windows were completely frosted over with ice, and all the jets could do was escort the plane, hoping to hear or see a flicker of life—something. Meanwhile, television and radio news got hold of the story, and millions of people were transfixed by the image of this ghostly, dark, silent plane flying through the sky with its escorts. Gradually, it veered more and more off course until, its fuel finally spent, it crashed in a field near Mina, South Dakota. There were no survivors. Authorities speculated that a sudden loss of pressure in the cabin had knocked everybody out, and the plane had simply flown on autopilot until it could fly no more.

By then, of course, we knew it was Payne, and the tears just flowed from both of us, and our thoughts and prayers immediately went to Tracey and their kids Chelsea and Aaron. The shock and pain would not go away. And then I thought of Payne's caddie, Mike Hicks, and his wife, Meg, and their children, and it occurred to me that Mike was probably on that plane as well. I immediately called my former caddie Mike Cowan—he was in Houston at the Tour Championship working for Tiger at the time—and asked him if he'd heard the news. And he said yes, that all the players down there had just heard about it. And I said, "Was Hicksie on the plane with him?"

And Fluff said, "No, Peter. He's standing right here with me."

And the next thing I knew Mike Hicks was on the phone talking to me, and the whole thing started to seem surreal. Mike had been walking off yardages on the Champions C.C. with Fluff, preparing for the tournament. And when Hicksie got on the phone, I just lost it. I was relieved that he was okay, but then we were talking about Payne, and we both went to pieces. Fluff told me later that he had to take care of Mike the rest of that day. Mike Hicks was Payne's best friend and caddie for about fifteen years.

Almost immediately I started getting calls from dozens of media outlets for comments about Payne and what he meant to the game, and that helped me to at least begin the healing process.

I WAS OVERWHELMED at the turnout for Payne's funeral in Orlando. Jan and I stayed with the O'Meara family, as did about four or five other couples. All of us arranged to go to the funeral together. There were over a hundred touring pros at his service, which was televised on ESPN. When Tracey got up and eulogized her husband, I was astonished at her courage. She was calm and composed and wonderful, and it was one of the bravest performances I've ever seen, for a woman to be able to do that when her man was taken from her so suddenly.

As the service was about to end, a priest came down and grabbed Greg Norman, who was sitting with us, and asked if all of the pros would form a line at the entrance of the church. He said, "If you guys get up there, everybody will follow." It turned out I was at the very front of the line, Greg was next to me, and Scott Hoch was across from us. After this amazing service that I'd cried all the way through, Tracey came around the pew and turned to head out of the church. She looked at me and just broke down crying, and so did I. I think it had been welling up in her through the service, but she'd been able to keep it together long enough to pay her special tribute, and then she just lost it.

She thanked me for being there, and then she saw Greg next to me. Greg and Payne had always had a fierce rivalry. They were two of the biggest names of the time, and two of the most engaging personalities, and both had large fan followings. Greg and Payne were sort of my generation's version of Nicklaus and Palmer. So Greg was crying also and he gave Tracey a big hug, and I just remember looking down that line and seeing Tom Lehman and Scott Hoch and Corey Pavin, and guys who'd gone head-to-head with Payne countless times and partnered with him in Ryder Cups. And Lee Janzen was perhaps the most emotional. He had twice beaten Payne in closing-stretch battles in U.S. Opens, in 1994 and 1998, and those competitions had formed a bond between them. All those things flashed through my mind that day, but casting a pall over all of it was that we all knew we'd never see Payne again, and that a loving young woman and her children were now without a husband and father, and there was no way to explain any of it.

His death has had a lasting impact on many of us. For months afterward I know that everyone on Tour felt closer. We're all independent contractors out there, and it's easy to go your own way and just kind of nod at other players and keep moving, but when I saw the other guys in the days after Payne's death, I noticed there was a lot more handshaking, and even a lot of hugging. We all seemed to appreciate one another more, and act more caring. The same thing happened on a national level after the tragedy of 9/11. Everyone seemed to drive slower on the highway, parents hugged their kids more often, and people waiting in line seemed to have more patience. It's a shame it takes a sudden death or a tragedy to make us all kinder and gentler, but that seems to be how it works.

In 2000, the year after he was killed, Payne would have been defending champion at two events at Pebble Beach, the AT&T and the U.S. Open. Like with so many of us, Pebble was one of Payne's favorite courses, and so I'll end with a story about that. At the 18th hole of Saturday's round at Spyglass Hill, Payne hit a four-iron a foot from the hole for birdie to take a one-stroke lead after fifty-four. The forecast was lousy for Sunday, so Payne knew there was a chance the final round would be rained out, which turned out to be the case.

Sunday came and it was raining cats and dogs, and I was sitting with Payne and Mike Hicks in the little locker room behind the pro shop on the first tee at Pebble. Payne was being interviewed by television and was asked to give his thoughts about the possibility of a rainout, which would give the title to him. Payne said all the right things. He said, "You know, you never want to win a tournament in a rainout. I really hope the weather clears and we get out there and play. It would be another chance to play my favorite course in the world, Pebble Beach, and I want to win this thing the right way."

The reporters turned and left, and I said to Payne, "So what do you really think about this weather?"

He gave me that devilish smile and said, "Rain, baby, rain."

2

Tinseltown and Big John

I MENTIONED THAT I won the U.S. Senior Open in 2004, and I'll have more about that later, but you should know that that wasn't my first major championship title—not if you count fiction along with fact. Anyone who saw the movie *Tin Cup* can tell you that, but for some reason nobody ever includes my nail-biting victory over Kevin Costner on my golfing résumé.

My first taste of Hollywood came in 1988, when I had a role in the HBO movie *Dead Solid Perfect,* based on a novel by Dan Jenkins. It was a tremendous artistic and emotional stretch for me, one that required years of method acting classes and a close study of the early work of Brando and Olivier: I was cast to play a professional golfer named Peter Jacobsen, who is trying to win the Colonial Invitational. It's pure coincidence that I actually have that same name in real life, and won that same tournament in 1984. And while it may seem like an easy role to play, it's actually not that easy trying to play yourself acting like yourself and acting like you're not in a movie when you actually are in a movie.

Anyway, it was a blast to be in—even if other actors got a few nude scenes and I was never asked—so when I was contacted eleven years later by John Norville, a Portland resident who'd written a golf script, and asked to play myself in his upcoming movie, I was interested. The movie was to be called *Tin Cup,* and would star Kevin Costner as a back-country golf professional with a world of talent but some bad habits that keep him from the big time—namely booze and broads.

As it turned out, several pros appeared in the film, including Craig Stadler, John Cook, Tommy Armour III, Lee Janzen, Jerry Pate, and others, and Gary McCord served as the technical adviser, whose primary task was to help Costner with his golf swing. He gave Kevin what appeared to be a fine swing and a lot of game, although both would fail the character, Roy McAvoy, at crunch time. But we'll talk about the movie's ending later. I should point out that the producers chose me to win the Open not because I was the likeliest candidate; I was picked simply because my playing schedule had me taking a week off from the Tour the same week they were filming the U.S. Open scenes down in Houston. But don't tell anyone I told you that. We'll keep that our little secret.

I was on the set of *Tin Cup* for about nine days, and was paid very well. But then money had nothing to do with my decision to participate. It just sounded like a lot of fun. The residual checks still dribble in years later, and can range anywhere from five hundred bucks to forty-three dollars and twelve cents.

I was completely impressed with Kevin Costner during my days on the shoot. He was a joy to work with, totally professional, and extremely nice to the crew and the extras. And for a guy whose handicap is probably somewhere between 6 and 10 depending on how much he's playing, I thought he did a credible job playing a guy who could contend in a U.S. Open.

One of the final scenes of the movie takes place on the 18th hole of the fictional Open. I was standing behind the director, Ron Shelton, observing the action, and Kevin had to identify a place from where, if he hit the shot solidly, he could barely get the ball to the green. That would set up the big final-hole gamble that would determine his fate. He chose a spot and said to Armour and Janzen and me, "Guys, do you think you can get there from here?"

We all kind of looked at one another, checked the yardage on the sprinkler head (it was about 215 yards), and then took out three-irons or four-irons and whipped balls onto the middle of the green.

Kevin took one look at those shots and said, "All right, it's time for lunch!"

We had a good laugh at that one.

In an earlier scene, I was on the green of a par-3 hole and had to putt up over a large rise. It was about a 35-footer. Costner and Don Johnson, who played another pro in contention to win, were standing back on the tee watching me. My holing the putt would then get a reaction from Costner, a line something like, "Jacobsen's making a move." The camera started out with a shot over the shoulders of Johnson and Costner watching me putt. On the green with me was my playing partner, Jerry Pate.

Shelton said, "Okay, here's the deal, Peter. You are going to hit this long putt up over this rise and into the cup. You are then going to turn and look back at Costner and Johnson and give a fist pump, sort of like, 'In your face, dude!'"

Well, that line might have worked in *Happy Gilmore,* but never in a million years would I do that for real. Maybe Sergio Garcia at age nineteen in a Ryder Cup match, but for me it was out of the question. I told Ron that, but he just said, "Whatever. Let's shoot it. Okay, ready, action, now set up over that putt, Peter, and knock it right in."

So I hit a long putt and it climbed up over the swale and just missed on the right edge. Shelton went, "Cut! Now, Peter, you've got to knock that thing in. Let's try it again."

And I said, "Time out, Ron. This is no easy putt. It's about a one-in-twenty-five shot. This may take a while."

And Ron said, "Well, we really have to get this shot in the can. We're rapidly losing light. Now knock it in!"

I quickly moved the ball to about 12 feet away, did one or two takes, and got the shot. But I remember saying to Shelton once we had it, "Ron, listen to me. If I could stand there and throw double-breaking, over-the-swale thirty-five-footers into the cup at will, I wouldn't be doing a small part in this friggin' movie. I'd own the entire studio."

I must say I loved the first ninety minutes of *Tin Cup*. I thought it had hilarious moments and I totally bought into the love story between the journeyman pro and his shrink, played by Rene Russo. I also got a big kick out of the volatile relationship between the pro and his caddie, played nicely by Cheech Marin. But the ending of the film has to go down as one of the most confusing in movie history. For those who might not have seen the film, the ten-thousand-to-one long-shot driving-range pro comes to the final hole of the U.S. Open with a chance to win, to realize a lifelong dream and nip this far more experienced professional named Peter Jacobsen. The hole is a par 5, and after a good drive, Costner's character, Roy McAvoy, elects to go for the green in two with a three-wood that must carry about 240 yards over water. Let's start with the fact that in my almost thirty years as a golf professional, I've never seen a screaming three-wood shot fly onto a green, roll up 3 feet short of the pin, and then stop and slowly start rolling back into the water. That's not going to happen at a U.S. Open, especially on a Sunday. If a green is that unfair—as actually happened in the second round of the U.S. Open at Olympic Club in

1998 (when Payne Stewart and others watched putts roll around the hole and then descend about 20 feet down the slope of the green) and on the 7th hole at Shinnecock Hills in the summer of 2004—tournament officials water it or raise the mower blades or choose a hole location that is more level.

But even if it were possible for a perfectly struck shot to roll back into the water, you must believe me on my gravestone when I tell you that any responsible Tour caddie who cared a whit about his player would not just walk but run on a dead sprint to the ball-drop area. Even with a penalty shot for going into the water hazard, the player would only be hitting his fourth shot and he would still have a good chance to save par. And if the player asked for the three-wood a second time, in order to try that same shot again, the caddie would snap it over his knee.

But in this Hollywood ending, with the gallery in awe, and Roy's girlfriend mumbling and pleading from behind the ropes, and Ken Venturi and Jim Nantz up in the announcer's booth expressing mock disbelief, Roy hit about seven more balls into the drink. And as if that weren't enough, on his final attempt, he knocks the ball in the hole and the crowd goes wild. What the crowd should have done is waved down an ambulance and had Roy carted away in a straitjacket to a cuckoo's nest.

When we were making the film, I had no idea that this was how it was going to end, or I would have pleaded with the director and producers to reconsider. It tainted what I otherwise thought was a really good movie.

That aside, I was extremely disappointed months later when I didn't garner an Oscar nod for my performance, not even a Golden Globe. After all, I've always been courteous to the foreign press. But it was kinda nice to bag a U.S. Open title. And if you don't believe it, then rent the DVD.

FOR ALL THE UNLIKELINESS OF THAT ENDING, however, we did have our own *"Tin Cup* moment" on the PGA Tour, featuring our very own version of Roy McAvoy, named John Daly. It took place in 1998 at Arnold Palmer's tournament at Bay Hill, on the 6th hole. Number 6 is a dogleg shaped from right to left with a pond guarding the left side. It's about 325 yards on the fly to clear the pond. No one had ever taken that route off the tee, so of course to please the fans John thought he'd give it a rip. He hit his first shot solid, but it splashed near the far end of the pond. With the fans urging him, John reloaded and tried again . . . and again . . . and again. He was going to make it come hell or high water, and he did eventually clear it, on about his sixth or seventh try. He ended up with an 18 on the hole. I think Arnold got a kick out of it because it was entertaining for the fans, and Palmer was never one to lay up himself.

As all golf fans know, Daly's career since he emerged from the shadows with his dark horse win in the 1991 PGA Championship has had more ups and downs and melodramatic moments than *As the World Turns.* At this writing, things seem to be on an upswing, and I hope they stay that way for him, because I truly like John and care about him as a person. I have so many stories about him that I'll begin with a recent one, but first a little background.

The third week in February 2004, I played in the Nissan Open at Riviera Country Club in Los Angeles, one of my favorite events on one of my favorite courses. I first fell in love with Riviera in 1983, when I came as close as I ever have to winning a major championship on the PGA Tour. I played the final round of the PGA Championship 7 under par through seventeen holes, and was tied with leader Hal Sutton as I stood on the 18th tee. A final bogey left me third alone, behind Sutton and Jack Nicklaus.

I also had fun there several years ago when I made a hole in one

on the 15th hole and won a new Nissan, which was on display behind the tee. I represented Toyota back then, but when the ball
rolled into the hole, I flipped off my Toyota visor before jumping
into the car, then grabbed the steering wheel and pretended that I
was going to drive it off the tee.

I did that so as not to ruin the moment for the Nissan people,
who may have wanted to use the videotape of the hole in one in future promotions. Later, a lot of players told me they couldn't
believe I had had such presence of mind. Maybe it's because my
company, Peter Jacobsen Productions, has been working closely
with corporations for years, and I've developed almost a protective
attitude about what works best for companies who put their money
behind the golf business. I instinctively knew that if I sat in the
driver's seat of a Nissan with Toyota emblazoned on my head, it
would embarrass Nissan and perhaps even get picked up by other
media as a slight to the tournament sponsor, and I just wasn't going to let that happen.

Anyway, I came into L.A. in 2004 with a lot of confidence. I'd
won more than $200,000 in the first four events, hadn't yet shot a
round over par, and would be playing a course I dearly loved. In
the back of my mind, I thought I had a reasonable chance to win.

As luck would have it, I was paired the first two rounds with
Big John, who just the week before at San Diego had won his first
tournament since the British Open in 1995. The long bunker shot
he nearly dunked on the first hole of sudden death, to beat Chris
Riley and Luke Donald, surely will go down as one of the shots of
the year.

When we wrote *Buried Lies* in 1992, Daly had just come onto
the scene, startling the golfing world by winning the 1991 PGA at
Crooked Stick after a series of withdrawals by players with ill-
nesses and one expectant wife (Nick Price's wife, Sue) allowed him
to enter at the last minute as the ninth alternate. It was the Cin-

derella story of the year, and golf fans everywhere embraced John as their everyman hero. He was a plain-talking, beer-swilling Arkansas boy, not quite a redneck, but certainly far removed from the stereotyped image of a stay-pressed touring pro.

But as we all know, this story was just beginning to unfold. My first business encounter was an arrangement with Daly at the end of 1992 to appear with Fuzzy Zoeller, Craig Stadler, and me in a one-day made-for-television event in Orange County called the Pro Stakes Challenge. It was to be televised on January 2, 1993, as a respite for golf fans who had had their fill of football bowl games and NFL playoffs. Well, just a week before the event we heard that John had allegedly pushed his wife into a wall in a domestic dispute in Colorado and would not be joining us.

We got Chi Chi Rodriguez to fill in at the last minute and the event came off fine, but it was a disappointing episode for John, the first of many over the next few years.

My scariest moment in over forty years of golf occurred during the Fred Meyer Challenge at Oregon Golf Club in 1993. We were conducting our annual Sunday clinic with celebrities and pros. It was an opportunity for ticket holders to be entertained by the top celebrities we had brought in, and to watch some shots and get some instruction from the best players in the world. We had set up a small stage with grass turf on the 18th green, facing back down the fairway, and the wind was coming up the valley and into our faces. The green was surrounded by grandstands and skyboxes, which were filled with patrons and sponsors and their kids. I had my partner Jack Lemmon on the pod entertaining the crowd, more with his personality and warmth than his golf shots, which can be hard to watch at times. It was early in the morning, about nine-fifteen, and Jack was still a little bound up. He hit one right, one left, and one fat. I looked over and there was John Daly with his Orca Killer Whale driver. I knew everyone wanted to see John blast a few down the fairway, so I called him over. But first I kidded Lemmon that his problem this morning was that he didn't have enough club, that he needed to try John's driver. Poor Jack took one swing with Daly's crowbar-shafted weapon with the fat head and nearly dislocated his shoulder. That got a big laugh. I then asked John to show the crowd how the Killer Whale was meant to be hit.

Daly had his ever-present cigarette and was sipping a Diet Coke. I remember he set a ball on the lip of the Coke can and took his first swing of the day. The result was a screaming snap hook—you might call it a giant shrimp—into the weeds. Then he did a slight shoulder stretch, teed up another ball, and hit it dead pure about 330 yards down the pipe. He suddenly turned to me and said, "You know, Peter, I hate hitting shots into the wind. I want to hit one downwind."

He reached into his pocket and pulled out a ball. Now, the year before at the clinic he had hit a chalk ball that exploded and got a big laugh, so when he teed up this ball from his pocket I assumed he was repeating the same gag. He waggled once, and then he stopped and leaned down and raised the tee slightly so the ball was sitting up higher. He aimed it at the top of the amphitheater, where there was a skybox and a makeshift radio station, and I said on the mike, "Why don't you take it right over the disk jockeys, so they'll have something to talk about on the air."

You must understand that John was no more than 20 to 25 feet from the first row of grandstand seats, where there were a bunch of kids, including my entire family. Jan was there, and our daughters Amy and Kristen, and son Mick. Without knowing it, John was actually aiming the shot right at my family. Mick, who was just eight years old, started scrambling for cover.

Jan said, "Relax, Mick, that is not a real ball. It's going to explode."

And Mick said, "No, Mom. It's got stripes on it," and he ducked. Sure enough, John ripped the thing and it came off the face super high and just barely cleared the top row of the grandstands. Jack Sheehan was helping me with the emcee duties and his memory is that the ball passed less than a foot over the head of a man with a crew cut. It would almost certainly have killed or seriously maimed anyone it struck in the head. We heard later that the ball landed in the tennis courts, about 300 yards away.

The crew we hired from ESPN was videotaping the clinic, and when you listen to the video and watch the tape of that moment, you see the ball take off like a shuttle launch and you can hear a collective gasp from the crowd. The people sat there frozen, not knowing what to think, obviously in disbelief. The lone voice you hear is Jack Lemmon's, because he was standing beside me and it was picked up on my microphone. "You've got the guts of a burglar," Lem said. And then I think I went into shock. If the ball had come off the club face one hundredth of an inch lower it would have taken off the head or body part of whomever it hit. And remember, this was only John's third swing of the day.

Now you must understand that this incident occurred in the first ten minutes of a one-hour clinic. I had fifty minutes of light-hearted entertainment to go. I whispered to Sheehan, "What should I say to the crowd?"

And Jack said, "Tell everyone in the third section that they will get a free dry cleaning at Frank's Laundromat."

I used the line and it got a pretty good response, sort of a nervous laugh. I think the crowd was still in disbelief at what they'd just witnessed.

Sheehan followed John back to his seat after "the shot heard 'round Portland," and he told me later that he asked John, "What the hell were you thinking?"

And John replied, "Oh, screw it. It was no big deal."

And Jack told him that under the circumstances, with lives on the line, it was the most amazing shot he'd ever seen.

And John said, "No, the most amazing shot I've ever hit was the one I hit out of Texas Stadium in a TV commercial."

And Jack said, "John, there was a huge difference."

And John said, "What's that?"

"Texas Stadium was empty," Jack said.

John paused for a second, took another pull on his smoke, and said, "I guess you're right."

I confronted John in the locker room after the clinic and just before the start of the pro-am. I said, "J.D., I can't believe you hit that shot. You could have killed somebody."

And he calmly replied, "But I didn't. I pulled it off."

I remember thinking, Yeah, well he did. It was either the most courageous shot I have ever seen hit or the most reckless, irresponsible thing I've ever seen. Years later I'm convinced it was the latter. But in a way the incident was character-revealing about John Daly, because I don't think John ever does anything out of ill will. His intent is never to hurt anybody, and he truly does love entertaining people. He teed up that ball without thinking about anything other than entertaining and amazing people with the shot. Weeks later, Tour Commissioner Deane Beman fined Daly $30,000 after John walked off the course in a pro-am in Hawaii. The Portland incident had clearly contributed to the amount of the fine.

And then there was the infamous moment at the British Open in 1994, when Daly made an offhanded comment to a reporter, complaining that he didn't understand why he got so much negative publicity about his drinking. John casually said that he wasn't the first guy on the PGA Tour to drink or use drugs. Naturally, there was a strong response from other players when they heard that one. Although he didn't mean it that way, it appeared that John had hurled a broadside at the entire Tour. I ended up sitting with Daly at a subsequent press conference to try to help him with damage control. But once the media grapevine circulates a hot quote like that, it's tough to stop the flood of negative reaction. Back in America, Curtis Strange, who was acting as the unofficial host of the Anheuser-Busch Golf Classic in Virginia, was asked on television to comment about Daly's remarks. And to paraphrase, Curtis said something like "John Daly ought to crawl back under that rock he climbed out from."

This, of course, gave the press some tasty gristle to chew on for the next several days, and the report of a two-time U.S. Open champion blasting a former PGA champion got wide play in the media. Ironically, the next time Strange and Daly would meet face-to-face was in an event that was designed to be lighthearted and entertaining. It was at the Merrill Lynch Shoot-Out on a Tuesday prior to the FedEx St. Jude Classic outside Memphis.

Jack Sheehan had been hired to emcee the Memphis event, but he had no idea who the participants would be until he arrived at the tournament. The field included defending champion Nick Price, Ben Crenshaw, Davis Love, and Fuzzy Zoeller, among others. The last two names on the pairing sheet were Curtis Strange and John Daly. Sheehan was concerned. As Jack said to me, "How are we supposed to turn this into a yuck-fest with these two guys in the same group? They've got to be hating each other's guts right now."

I thought it was funny and said something like "That's why they pay you the big bucks, Jack. If it was easy, anybody could do it."

And I remember Mike Cowan, who was caddying for me then, telling Jack he should just ignore the situation and pretend like nothing had transpired between the two guys.

"Yeah, but I've asked other players in the Shoot-Out and they say I can't ignore it," Jack said. "Besides, they've written up the story behind this pairing in the morning paper. Fuzzy said they have a plan that will get a big laugh."

And Fluff Cowan said, "I don't know, Jack. Curtis can be pretty thin-skinned at times."

Fluff and I were on the putting green, and after about forty-five minutes, Jack came back over and wanted to discuss the plan some more. Fuzzy Zoeller had concocted an idea that he thought would defuse the tension between Strange and Daly and get a big laugh from the gallery. He would set a rock beside the 10th tee, where the Shoot-Out would begin, and place a towel over it. Then, when Jack announced John Daly, Fuzzy would lift up the rock and ask John to crawl out and hit his drive. Jack said he thought it was a good idea, as long as Fuzzy was the instigator, but ten minutes later Fuzzy came over and said he was dropping out of the Shoot-Out because his back was hurting. This would leave the prank entirely up to Sheehan to execute, and he wasn't at all certain he should do it. Fuzzy said, "If you have one single hair on your ass, Jack, you'll do it. Let's pump a little life into this affair."

Price and Love and Crenshaw all encouraged Jack to go ahead with it. They said they thought it would be a hoot. Fluff stuck by his guns and said if it were him, he wouldn't do it.

Well, when the moment came and Jack was about to introduce Daly, he got down on his knees and removed the towel from the rock. On the mike, and in a loud voice, he asked John to crawl out and hit his drive. Just as he was doing that, Daly dumped a 32-ounce Gatorade on Sheehan's back. Now Memphis in July is as humid as it gets, so Sheehan's shirt looked like it had been dipped in cement. But the fashion disaster was the least of his concerns as Curtis reacted to what he felt had been a bow shot against him.

As they left that first tee, Curtis was walking next to Crenshaw, who had a lavalier microphone attached to his shirt so the crowd could enjoy his comments. Instead of the gentle banter of Gentle Ben, the gallery heard Curtis fuming, "What the f——is this? I said something two weeks ago and I'm eating f——ing sh—— for it every day! This is f—— bullsh——!" He was dropping more F-bombs than a Sam Kinison–Andrew Dice Clay double bill.

Meanwhile, Jack had three more hours with these guys to lighten the mood and make everything seem like it was fun and games. He told me it was like cracking jokes at a funeral. Everybody just felt bad and wanted to go home.

The episode ended up as the headline in the Memphis newspaper the next day, and the article recounted how the rock joke had backfired on Sheehan.

John Feinstein even included the story in his book *A Good Walk Spoiled*. As for Sheehan, he retired from emceeing Shoot-Outs after that day and returned to his full-time career as a writer.

But to underscore all of this, let me say that like millions of golfers, I, too, am a fan of John Daly's. I think he's a good guy, that he's a great asset to the PGA Tour, and I'm delighted that he seems to have confronted some of his demons and gotten his life back on track. His golf game certainly has recovered fully. In my two rounds with Long John at the Nissan Open, he made fourteen birdies, shot 68–64, and had the crowds cheering wildly for every shot. He ended up fourth for the week, winning $230,000. In just those two weeks in Southern California, he won about $1.1 million and clearly showed that his game was back on track and that he would once again be a force every time he teed it up. John is such an amazing talent, and such a character, that he adds a lot of energy to the entire package of the PGA Tour. We hear too much about the cookie-cutter personalities of the guys on Tour. Nobody can ever put that rap on Big John.

3

Plugged In

PROFESSIONAL GOLF IS so different from other big-time sports in that there is no generally accepted time to retire from competition. In football, thirty-five is considered ancient. The only guys who last much past that are drop-back quarterbacks or placekickers. In baseball and basketball, forty is considered antiquated. Roger Clemens and Michael Jordan could still get it done past the big four-oh, but they are exceptional athletes who kept their bodies in peak condition year-round. In tennis, Andre Agassi is pushing the envelope at thirty-five, and Pete Sampras, who won more major titles than anyone, hung it up at thirty-two.

But in golf, I don't think we fully understand the age limits. When you consider that, in 1998, Jack Nicklaus finished sixth in the Masters, at age fifty-eight, and in 1974, Sam Snead finished second in the Los Angeles Open at sixty-one, it's obvious that the lifespan of professional golfers can approach that of land turtles. Heck, Vijay Singh set the all-time single-season earnings title last year by winning over $10 million at age forty-one!

The first time I wondered whether I was ready to pull back the reins on a full-time competitive career on the PGA Tour was in

1992, when I signed a deal with the sports division at ABC to provide color commentary on ten broadcasts in the 1993 season. I was thirty-eight years old and coming off a disappointing season in which I'd lost my father and temporarily lost my passion to compete. While I didn't feel that I was washed up, I was unhappy with my play and I knew that opportunities to get a major network commentary job didn't come along every day. I've always enjoyed new challenges and when this one presented itself—even though it was an extremely difficult decision—I decided to take it. I would be partnering with Brent Musberger, one of the very best in the business and a great guy, and I viewed it as an opportunity to scratch a creative itch and share some opinions with the golfing public.

My year went well, I thoroughly enjoyed myself, but there were a few philosophical differences that suggested to me that maybe my personality didn't totally jibe with the guiding philosophy of ABC's golf producers. One quick story to illustrate:

In the 1993 British Open at Royal St. George's, our broadcast crew of Musberger, Jerry Pate, Mark Rolfing, Judy Rankin, Peter Alliss, and Steve Melnyk was having a great time. I had never been able to enjoy the Open from the sidelines, as it were, so I did some mingling with the gallery, got a great feel for the atmosphere, and did some serious chowing down at the food huts.

There was a food stand called the Jacket Potato, with terrific coleslaw and incredible baked potatoes with creamed corn and baked beans poured over them. I couldn't get enough of them, and whenever we had shift breaks from our coverage—because the British Open telecasts basically last all day—Brent and I would go down and scarf the potatoes and beans and soak up the atmosphere. The combination of those wonderful delicacies found me taking more bathroom breaks than normal, if you catch my drift.

On Sunday, Greg Norman was on his way to a convincing win

by shooting a final-round 64 when suddenly, out of nowhere, our cameras turned to a Porta Potti off to the side of the 18th hole that was ablaze. I mean the flames were licking up to the sky, and there were people running in every direction away from it. Musberger, who's the consummate old pro and very quick on his feet, said, "The only thing hotter than Greg Norman right now is that outhouse." It was a good line, so I wanted to add another and here's what came out. "You know, Brent, I knew that selling all those baked beans around the golf course was a bad idea."

Brent giggled, but there was no laughter coming from my headphones. It was one of about fifty times that year that I got scolded for my "colorful" commentary.

At the end of the '93 season, I had enjoyed my experience in the booth, but I was licking my chops to get back to a full-time playing schedule. I also hoped to do more television work in the future, as long as it was a comfortable fit for my competitive schedule.

I HAD KNOWN DAVE MANOUGIAN for several years before he was named CEO of the Golf Channel. In the early eighties, Dave was the national sales manager for Nike, at a time when a guy named Ric Long and I built the first golf shoe for Nike. We put it together with components from shoes used in basketball, baseball, and tennis, and just added golf spikes.

I remember the day we walked into Nike chairman Phil Knight's office and dropped the shoe on his desk. He said, "What's this?"

"It's a golf shoe," I said. "Golf is the next sports division for Nike."

"We will never be in golf," Phil said. "I don't like golf. It's boring."

I said, "No offense, Phil, but it doesn't matter that you hate golf, because everyone else loves it. What do you think Michael Jordan and Charles Barkley and so many of the top Nike athletes do when they're not competing in their main sport? They play golf. And what do you think all the CEOs and executive VPs and marketing executives you deal with do on weekends? They play golf. Golf is going to be a huge business for your company."

I was well aware that Phil Knight—like me, a University of Oregon grad—had started Nike with a waffle-soled track shoe invented by himself and Oregon track coach Bill Bowerman, so Ric and I thought it fitting that a new golf division should also be launched with a shoe. And that day marked the unofficial start of Nike's involvement in golf. I agreed to wear the Nike prototype shoe even though I wasn't getting paid to do it. I wore it for about a year, and Ric and I constantly made changes and improvements. I knew it had to be a helluva shoe for Tour players to wear and endorse it.

After another year, Nike officially formed a golf division and paid me $5,000 to wear the shoe and the Nike swoosh on my shirts. I was the first and only golfer under contract to them. It went along that way for about three years, and then Mark Bisbing came to be in charge of the division and saw the potential for a larger product line for golf clothing. Seve Ballesteros and Curtis Strange were signed to wear the Nike shoes and shirt, and it was a great marketing coup when Curtis won back-to-back U.S. Opens in 1988 and '89. He gave a face to our efforts. Then, of course, when Phil Knight signed Tiger to a huge contract the day he turned pro in 1996, Nike Golf was suddenly a major player in the industry. Today, there are probably forty to fifty golfers on the PGA Tour alone who represent Nike, and I'm proud of the role I played in that, especially because it's an Oregon-based company.

BUT BACK TO MY FRIENDSHIP with Manougian. I was having breakfast with Dave at Clint Eastwood's Mission Ranch during the

AT&T National Pro-Am in 2001 when we started talking about what I might do for the Golf Channel. I explained the pros and cons of my broadcast stint at ABC, and I knew I didn't want to be trapped in the booth for a long-term commitment that would detract from playing tournament golf. However, I told Dave that if I could stretch my muscles a little and maybe create my own show that would emphasize the fun aspects of the game, I would be interested.

He said, "You've got a deal," and we signed a contract and created the show. From the beginning it was called *Plugged In with Peter Jacobsen*. Our show would combine music, humorous skits, offbeat features, and commentary on current issues or personalities in golf. As we were putting together the format, I wanted Matt Griesser for a cohost, a young comedian who was becoming familiar to golf fans as Sign Boy, the quirky character in the FootJoy commercials. I thought the campaign he was fronting was hilarious. Matt played sort of a foot-fetishist who idolized the players, almost with a stalker's fervor. He would sniff their shoes in the locker room, knew the sizes of their gloves, and even had all the product numbers for the shoe models memorized. He was the ultimate golf groupie, albeit a touch twisted. The campaign was very edgy stuff for the world of professional golf, but it was working and FootJoy's sales were huge.

I told Dave that I wanted to use Matt as my cohost and sidekick. He could carry the humor side of things and still let me be me, and we would create skits that would give the Golf Channel a little more energy and a slightly younger demographic. I thought he would be a good comic foil for me, sort of like the George Costanza character that Jason Alexander played opposite Jerry Seinfeld (not that I'm trying to compare *Plugged In* to *Seinfeld,* but you get the idea).

The response was that the producers didn't feel they needed

anybody but me on the show. Certainly part of their reasoning was that they didn't know Matt like I did. But when the producers came to appreciate his versatility and talent, they agreed to my request.

Our first skit was sort of a *Candid Camera* stunt. We set up a card table in front of a store called Golf Headquarters, in Cedar Hills, Oregon. My golf bag with my name on it was beside the table, and a sign that looked like a fourth-grader had written it said: "Golf Tips $1 . . . by a Pro."

People would walk over to the table and ask what I was doing. I'd tell some of them that I was giving tips and that I was keeping the money. Others I would tell that I was giving the money to charity. I introduced Matt as my manager and the head instructor in my academy. If the person forked over a buck for the tip, I would tell Matt what I wanted him to impart to the student, and then I would leave and go inside. As soon as I did, Matt would trash me to the guy and tell him I really wasn't very knowledgeable about the golf swing. He would say, "Ya know Peter is really a fine player. He's beaten the best players in the world many times. But he absolutely sucks as an instructor. He really doesn't know much at all about the golf swing."

When I'd come back out and ask for a report, Matt would say something like, "Oh, your advice was awesome, Peter. I think it will really help his game." The whole shtick was based on the double takes we'd get from the unsuspecting students.

Then Matt would take this old wedge out of my bag—one that had been put in there just for the skit—and he'd demonstrate a swing and whack the wedge on the pavement, and I would get all pissed off that he was damaging my equipment.

At one point I said to a gentleman who walked out of the store, "Do you want a golf lesson?"

He said, "No, I hit the ball well, but I can't putt." So I said, "The most important thing we've got to do with putting is minimize the hand action. You want to let your arms hang loosely at your sides."

"I use a cross-handed method," my new student said. The man started to show me this jerky cross-handed move. I remembered that I had a belly putter I'd been experimenting with in the car, so I got it out. "Let me show you something that is really big right now in Europe," I said. "It's perfect for taking the hands and arms out of the stroke." And I stuck the grip end of the belly putter in my mouth and started swaying my head back and forth to create a putting stroke. I then tried to say, "See how good this works," but it came out "whee-ow-goog-i-weer."

And then Matt grabbed the putter right out of my mouth and put it in his own piehole without cleaning off the drool, which is the hygienic equivalent of taking a swig from a guy's Coke after he's just released three ounces of backwash into it. Our student looked a tad grossed out by that, but then Matt proceeded to tell the guy, with the gooey end of the putter in his kisser, that I had used the "oral stroke" to make a five-footer on the last hole at Colonial to make the thirty-six-hole cut right on the number. The hardest part about these skits is not busting up when your partner is throwing some great ad-lib out there, especially when you've got the hook set deep in the "student's" lip and you don't want to ruin the take.

This poor guy was buying the routine and he just had to try the oral stroke. So he took the putter from Matt and sort of nonchalantly—so as not to hurt his feelings—wiped the top off on his sleeve and then stuffed the grip in his own mouth. I didn't dare look at Matt or I knew I'd lose it. Not only was the guy getting the most bogus golf lesson in history, but he'd just contracted whooping cough and hoof-and-mouth disease.

So that was our first effort for the Golf Channel, and viewers responded. We were encouraged to dream up more sophomoric stunts. It was like asking the brattiest kid in school to enter a burping contest.

ONE YEAR WE DECIDED to do a *Plugged In* Christmas show in Portland, so I got dressed as Santa and Matt as my elf. (This was before Will Ferrell brought elf-dom to a whole new level on the big screen.) Matt wore a green suit that looked like Kermit the Frog on steroids. We went to a first-grade classroom and I told stories, but they weren't about reindeer or Santa's workshop, they were all about golf. Which confused the kids because they didn't know that Santa was a golf freak. I would say to a little girl, "How did you like that Callaway driver I brought you last year?" And she would say, "Are you crazy? You brought me Barbie dolls."

Then we went to a nine-hole executive course and sat on a bench on a par-3 hole. When the golfers would first walk up, pulling their handcarts, they would think, Ah, that's nice that someone has hired a Santa to spread the Christmas spirit. But I would tell them that actually I had been hired by the course owners to hit their shot on that hole. They'd think I was kidding until I teed it up and knocked it on the green. And they'd be impressed that Santa actually had a little game.

Then I baited them a little and asked, "Are there any really good golfers that live in Portland? I mean, does Tiger Woods or Phil Mickelson live here? Santa needs to know because I have to decide if they are naughty or nice and whether I need to deliver them a present."

One of the older gentlemen finally took the hook and said, "Nobody any good lives here. Well, Peter Jacobsen lives here."

I said, "Santa needs to know if this Peter is a good player."

The old-timer said, "He used to be good, but he's not good anymore."

I said, "Really. Why isn't he any good anymore?"

He said, "Well, you know, he's getting older and the muscles and bones don't work too good anymore."

At that point I whipped off the beard and the guy wanted to die, he was so embarrassed. He kept apologizing, but I explained that his reaction was exactly what we were looking for, and of course he said, "No, please. I really do think you're a good player." It was classic.

After we did the golf course gig, Santa and his elf were driving back to the clubhouse and I smelled like a backed-up septic tank. That suit was very hot, and I'd been hitting golf shots and bouncing around and it was getting gamey in there. Suddenly we saw a little girl, about five years old, in the neighborhood that bordered the golf course. She saw Santa and her eyes bugged out of her head. My elf Griesser said, "Dude, look at those eyes. She's awestruck. We've got to go back so you can be Santa for her."

I said, "No, man, I'm tired. Santa wants to call it a wrap."

He said, "No, dude, you'll make her whole year. You need to do it right, and not reveal your true identity."

So we went back and I did the whole routine with her. She told me her name was Sammy Jo. I picked her up, I held her in my arms, and her mom was standing in the front yard, beaming. I started singing "Rudolph the Red-Nosed Reindeer," and Sammy Jo sort of pulled away like I was invading her space, and I was thinking my breath must stink like I'd been eating bad Limburger, but I kept up the act. Finally, after a few minutes I put her down, and I saw Grandma come hustling out of the garage. She was right out of *The Beverly Hillbillies,* false-teeth division, and she was hunched over, braless, wearing a tank top, and you could tell that she used to be like a 44C, but now was a 36 long. Her bosoms were bouncing off the waistband of her shorts, and she had huge meaty alligator upper arms.

In the deepest, raspiest voice I've ever heard (think Linda Blair in *The Exorcist*), she said, "Oh my God, it's Santa! Oh God, how wonderful!"

She then put her face right in mine, and I was thinking it's a draw as to whose breath was worse, and she said, "Fantastic. Merry Christmas, Santa." I pulled back faster from her than Sammy Jo had from me. Then she leaned down and said, "Sammy Jo, honey, it's Santa Claus. Didja *hug* him? Didja *hug* him?"

Sammy Jo looked as scared as I was, and I was scared shitless. We're talking about a real crypt-keeper here.

We were finally able to break away, and after what seemed like days I got out of that damn Santa suit, but in thirty seconds Granny had managed to provide our crew with the catchphrase for the rest of the season on *Plugged In*. I couldn't bump into any of our guys anywhere without them dropping their voices about two octaves and going, "Didja *hug* him?"

ANOTHER GOLF CHANNEL stunt occurred in the fall of 2004 in Eugene, on the University of Oregon campus, where I'm about three classes short of graduation, but that's another story. It involved the popular bar game Golden Tee Golf, but before I share the Golf Channel prank story, a little background is necessary. In the early 1990s, a group from Incredible Technologies and Bulldog Entertainment came to me with a new idea to incorporate golf with alcohol consumption. You're probably thinking, Wow, there's a novel idea. But actually it was. I was involved in the process of developing the game, which was about the shape of a pinball machine. It requires the player to spin a recessed ball, which sticks halfway out of the top panel, and then with the palm of the hand propel the ball forward to simulate hitting a golf shot. The player's force on the ball determines the distance of the shot, and the degree of sidespin left or right determines the amount of hook or fade. During the early development of the game, I went into a studio, where they put light sensors and little reflector balls on my head and arms, elbows and legs, and took tons of high-tech photos so that the little animated Peter (make sure you capitalize the *P* there) in the game would replicate my exact golf swing. Then Pat Summerall and I taped a variety of comments that would be used to describe various results. For example, if someone hit a shot in the water, my voice in the game would say, "Would you like a little Scotch with that water?" Another poor result might elicit a comment such as, "Man, you need to head to the practice tee."

Little did I know when this game was developed that it would become a national phenomenon, and that a whole pack of bar rats all around the country would know Peter Jacobsen more for his being the Golden Tee guy than for anything he'd done on a real golf course. For years now, they've held big Golden Tee tournaments all over the country, where people can win up to $50,000. Some people have quit their jobs to become full-time Golden Tee professionals. There are even interactive games between cities, so someone in Omaha can compete against a stranger in Seattle. I've been asked to appear at a couple of their national conventions to hand out checks to the winners of tournaments. Pretty wild.

I can't resist telling one on my daughters, Kristen and Amy. Several years ago, Amy was a student at Syracuse University and Kristen was at NYU, and they were both in a New York bar, underage, and using fake IDs. They were with a bunch of friends, had just ordered a cocktail, and all of a sudden they heard my voice saying, "It's great to be here, Pat."

Amy said, "Oh my God, Kristen! Dad's here." They both ducked under the table, thinking I was going to bust them right there. It so happened that their booth was right next to a Golden Tee machine, and my voice shocked them.

Back to our prank in Eugene. It was after the first football game of the year for the Oregon Ducks and we went to The Cooler, a bar near Autzen Stadium, which we knew would be packed with UO students. I was with Matt Griesser. We put a hidden camera behind the Golden Tee game, and Matt and I sat in a van outside the joint, with microphones. Obviously, many of the students playing the game had been enjoying beverages all afternoon, so it was very easy to mess with them. Here's how it went down:

A student would put a dollar in the machine, and from the van I would say, "Hi, everybody. Welcome to Golden Tee. I'm Peter Jacobsen, your host. And joining me as always is Matt Griesser. Matt, good to have you with me again."

Matt would say, "Thanks, Peter. I'm not wearing any pants."

And the students would look up and say something like, "What did he say?" Then they'd laugh and keep playing.

A guy would hit a bad shot, and I'd say. "Ouch. That was terrible. It's obvious this guy has never played before."

Matt would say, "Yeah, and look at the T-shirt he's wearing. Check out those stains. It's obvious this dude eats standing over a sink."

The poor guy with mustard on his shirt would stand there shocked, wondering how the hell this machine could get so personal.

Or we might hear a guy say, "Hey, Bill. Let's play."

And Matt would say, "Yeah, c'mon, Bill. You can't suck as bad as Tom."

The students would go, "Cool! It knows our names!"

There was an attractive girl standing near the game, wearing beads like the ones they hand out on Bourbon Street during Mardi Gras. Tom would whack the ball, and Matt would say, "Quit whacking me, Tom. Let the chick with the beads play." Of course, the girl with the beads started getting all self-conscious that she was getting this attention.

There was one guy who would swear at the game. He'd hit a bad shot and say, "Aw, f——!"

Matt would say, "Two-shot penalty for profanity."

The guy would go, "F—— you" back to the machine.

And Matt would say, "Make that four shots."

The amazing thing is that they never did figure out the prank . . . which may say more about the average SAT scores of those students than anything else.

My daughter Amy was there, and after we'd messed with the students awhile she would bring them outside to our van and show them how they'd been "punked." They would say, "Oh, dude! We *knew* something fishy was going down."

EASILY THE MOST REWARDING SHOW we've done on *Plugged In* was in May 2003, when we visited the American troops stationed at Guantánamo Bay. We went down there at the request of a golfer friend of mine, Mike Heard, who is with the FBI. I took Matt Griesser and my son Mick and we brought along Hootie and the Blowfish, plus a bunch of goodies for the troops, like baseball mitts and bats donated by the "Big Unit," Randy Johnson, guitars donated by the Gibson company, and tons of golf clubs and other equipment from Nike, Titleist, Taylor Made, Callaway, and Ping. We packed all of it on a C-130T transport plane, which is about the most uncomfortable aircraft you can ever fly as a passenger. There were just a bunch of hammock slings for your ass. It was about a two-hour flight from Jacksonville to the tip of Cuba, where Guantánamo Bay is located.

We spent three days there, visiting every branch of the service—Navy, Army, Air Force, Marines, and Coast Guard. They all serve one purpose or another down there and do a magnificent job.

We visited the camp where the Al Qaeda prisoners and enemy combatants from Afghanistan were being held, and I can tell you the Army soldiers who were guarding them were studs. They were red-white-and-blue tough hombres, the kind you definitely want on your side in any fight. I felt reassured knowing those men and women have our back.

The military had a little nine-hole makeshift golf course there and we held a pseudo–celebrity pro-am, and then a clinic in which Griesser and I screwed around and I did some impressions. That's when we announced that we were giving them all the golf equipment and baseball gear. I then made an unofficial announcement that even though I hadn't received the proper authority, I was officially renaming the nine-hole golf course in the sand, with five-foot iguanas crawling everywhere, the TPC at Guantánamo Bay, and these guys gave us a huge cheer. It was an enlightening three days and an experience I'll always remember.

A Breakout Year

As I mentioned, when I spent much of 1993 in the broadcast booth, there was some speculation that I might be phasing out as a player and going into a second career in broadcasting. I don't believe in my gut I ever thought that was the case. There were a lot of reasons for the move into the booth—some golf-related, some not.

I had not played well in 1992, and for the first time in my career had finished out of the top 125 on the money list. Even though I still had most of the necessary exemptions to play a full schedule in 1993, my mind was not totally on golf. I had the book offer to write *Buried Lies,* and my golf-course architectural business was starting to get off the ground, but most important I was concerned about my father Erling's declining health. He had been battling cancer of the larynx and tongue for a few years and was getting weaker by the month.

Erling Jacobsen died on July 1, 1992, the family with him at the end, and his passing just broke our hearts and my spirit. My dad was the one who introduced me to golf, taught me how to hold a club, taught me how to control my temper and turn aggression into a positive force, and most important taught me that golf is a game to be enjoyed and is an ideal platform on which to build life-long friendships and business relationships. Basically, all the essential ingredients that a young golfer needs to learn were instilled in me by my father, and when he left us, my desire to compete was diminished for a time. That was reflected by my indifferent play for about a year, and when ABC started courting me in the fall of '92 to work in the broadcast booth, I accepted their offer because I needed a diversion, and I'd always wanted to try my hand at television.

Golf is really the only sport that has no off-season. We go anywhere from forty-four to forty-eight weeks a year, choosing our one- or two-week breaks along the way, but there's never a sustained period in a professional golfer's life when he can kick back and assess his life and his goals both on and off the course. As 1992 came to a close, I knew my passion for the sport was at low tide, and for the first time since I had turned professional in 1976 I questioned how long I wanted to battle with the intensity and commitment required to play the PGA Tour at a high standard.

Inspiration to play at that level has to come from a variety of sources, but it mainly has to come from deep within and from a pure love of the game. And it has to come from a commitment to getting it right, which is exhibited by players like Jack Nicklaus and Vijay Singh and Tiger Woods. Those guys have an obsession with wanting to do things right in their golf swings and short games. That's why you see them beating balls at the end of the range and spending hours around the practice green chipping and putting long after other players have called it a wrap. And that's why you see them making swing changes even when they seem to be playing flawless golf. The golfing world was more than surprised when Tiger made dramatic swing changes with Butch Harmon not long after winning the Masters by twelve strokes in 1997.

And although those changes kept him from being at the top of his game for close to eighteen months, when it all clicked he went on a five-year tear that produced the best golf that has ever been played. Reaching the pinnacle of our sport requires a search for perfection at a very difficult game, even though we all know that perfection is not possible.

Although I still played in twenty-three Tour events in 1993 despite a broadcasting schedule that called for ten weekends in the booth, I found that every time I analyzed other players going down the stretch, I missed being in the action myself. I knew that this TV deal with ABC was not marking my move into retirement, as some people thought, but rather was a necessary hiatus to recharge my battery and enhance my commitment to my profession.

When I decided to curtail my broadcasting duties at the end of the 1993 season, the main reason was that I wanted to commit myself totally to doing it right again. So I started to work more closely with my teacher and business partner Jim Hardy to get my golf swing where I wanted it. Hardy's theories on golf regarding the one-plane and two-plane swings, described in detail in his book *The Plane Truth for Golfers,* explain with great clarity what I was working on. I was Jim's sounding board for those theories, which have propelled him into recognition as one of the top teachers in the game. We all try to make a flawless swing every time, but it doesn't happen and literally *cannot* happen. Still, we can move closer to flawless by careful analysis and hard work. And I was committed in late '93 to doing just that. Let me explain the changes we made:

Growing up and in my early years on Tour, I had always had a two-plane golf swing. But a two-plane swing demands that you rely on rhythm, tempo, timing, and balance. If that's not there, you're in trouble. Hardy felt we needed to develop a one-plane swing, in which the shoulders and arms swing around the trunk on the same plane, much like a baseball player swinging at a pitch, except of course that the golfer is more bent over, in order to hit the ball off the ground rather than at chest level. A two-plane swinger stands taller to the ball, and turns his hips and shoulders fairly level to the ground, but swings his arms up and down somewhat vertically; in other words, he uses two different planes.

Hardy and I worked on getting my arms behind my body more on the backswing. By contrast, a two-planer can't have his arms behind him or he's in big trouble. He must have them in front of his body. An example of a one-plane baseball player who is also a one-plane golfer is Mark McGwire, and as a result he has great power at both. He can hit a 95-mile-per-hour fastball out of the stadium and a golf ball out of a round with one swing. Most two-planers are not power players, but are very accurate. Payne Stewart and Scott Simpson represent the two-plane swing. There are exceptions— two-planers who can really move it, like Tom Watson and Davis Love III, but when a two-planer is struggling with his tempo, timing, rhythm, or balance, it's time to holler, "Fore!"

We also worked on turning my body and arms immediately left on the follow-through. Two-planers try to keep the club head "down the line," which results in the arms swinging more vertically. That move is a disaster for the one-planer. We emphasized a steeper shoulder turn on the backswing, keeping my shoulders turning at a 90-degree angle to my spine at the top of my swing, which is essential for a one-planer, and then continuing that 90-degree relationship throughout the golf swing.

Although my game didn't come together quickly, and 1994 turned out to be a mediocre year for me (eighty-eighth on the money list), I knew I was making progress toward playing really well. I recall giving Hardy hell for not making it through the Senior Tour qualifying tournament, and he fired back with, "Peter, if I could get inside your body, I'd win three or four times, and maybe that's because I'm a meaner son of a bitch than you are." He told me that by March or April of '94 I had a solid swing going, but that I didn't know it yet and didn't appreciate how close I was to breaking out of mediocrity. Jim said to ignore all the critics who said the reason my playing record wasn't more sterling was because of my outside interests. He said that the reason I hadn't won more was because I never quite had the total mechanics to win, that I would hit too many bad shots at the wrong time.

I also received a lot of help from Dave Pelz, who for years had told me that I had the potential to be a top player if I'd concentrate on my short game. So what do you suppose Dave did when I called him and asked for help? He flat out turned me down. I emphasized that I was really serious about it this time, and he said, "No, you're not. I've known you too many years. You're a lot of words and a lot of lip service. You're a great guy, but I don't want to waste our time." Dave even told *Golf World* magazine that although I had the ability "to learn anything I teach him in about three and a half seconds, he can also forget it and try something new in another three and a half seconds." He said, "Peter is the most distractible person I've ever seen. If there is anyone else around, Peter will talk to him."

Chuck Hogan, another of my longtime friends and instructors, made a similar comment to Gary Van Sickle of *Golf World*. Chuck said he would run into instructors all the time who claimed to have given me lessons. "Well, no shit," Hogan said. "Who hasn't given Peter their two cents' worth? He'd listen to flies going by."

While this was a moderate exaggeration, there was some truth to what he said, so I resolved to put in earplugs and not listen to anyone other than Hardy and Pelz, who finally, after a ritual of begging, actually did take me on. And when he did, I got the results I wanted. Dave discovered that I was missing putts on the low side of the cup 85 percent of the time, and that I seldom read enough break. He also got me to use more of a stroke than a hit on both chips and putts. By implementing his advice, I saw positive results in my short game in the latter half of the '94 season.

I also spent a good portion of 1994 working out with a personal trainer in Portland, a talented guy named Fil Pearl. Jan knew him from a health club he worked at. I bumped into him in a Safeway early in the year, and I was looking a tad heavy and probably buying bags of Chips Ahoy! cookies and Krispy Kreme doughnuts at the checkout stand. He yelled over to me that we needed to start a workout program. I remember feeling that he was absolutely right. That meeting occurred just prior to the '94 Masters, because I remember working out while the tournament was on TV, and Fil said he could see in my eyes how disappointed I was that I hadn't qualified for Augusta. We got on a great program requiring several workouts a week that lasted close to two hours each. I'd spend one hour on weights and forty-five minutes to an hour on cardiovascular conditioning. During the months I was with Fil, my weight dropped from 225 pounds to 204. Swing-wise, body-image wise, and with a renewed desire to play great golf, I started the 1995 season with the best attitude I'd had in years.

I missed the cut in my second tournament, the Phoenix Open, by one shot, then headed to Pebble Beach for what has always been a very special event for me. I knew I was right on the edge of putting everything together. I was hitting the ball well and putting well. Golf was fun again. And the most enjoyable week of the year for me every year is the AT&T National Pro-Am at Pebble Beach. Once again, I would partner with my dear friend Jack Lemmon, whom I called the Human Hinge, and try my darnedest to help us make the final-day cut in the pro-am competition for the first time. For the umpteenth time, we fell just short, missing the fifty-four-hole cut by only one stroke, but after a third-round 66, I found myself just one shot out of the individual tournament lead. I was hitting the ball as well as I ever had, making my share of putts, and felt extremely relaxed. Although I hadn't won in just over five years, since the 1990 Bob Hope Chrysler Classic, my nerves were steady and my tempo and golf swing were right where I wanted them. And with the final round of the three-course rotation being played at Pebble Beach, I was on my favorite course and one I know as well as any on the Tour.

Lemmon came along and walked the first three holes of the final round with me, but I knew he had to get back to L.A. to start rehearsals for a new movie he was doing. I believe it was *Grumpier Old Men,* with his sidekick Walter Matthau. When I birdied the first three holes, he said, "You've got this well in hand, partner. When I get out of my car in L.A., I expect to see you on the 18th green holding that trophy." Jack's words gave me even more encouragement, but unlike football, where a linebacker may bang his head against his locker six times to get fired up before going out on the battlefield, a golfer must do everything possible to keep the heart rate steady. On that particular day, I knew my golf swing was about where I wanted it, my short game felt good, but my mind was roving all over the place, simply because of all the memories I had of Pebble Beach.

When I was a kid growing up in Portland, during spring break our family used to jump in the station wagon and drive down to Pebble Beach. We'd all carry our clubs on our backs and play thirty-six holes. Those were wonderful memories. Sure, like any family we had our disagreements and our spats, but we all loved and respected one another. As I played that last nine holes, I couldn't help thinking that I now had lost my brother Paul to AIDS, and my father Erling to cancer, and that I was trying to win for them. I was getting the job done, despite all those waves of nostalgia washing over me, but the guys right behind me, who happened to be Davis Love and David Duval, were making birdies right along with me and I remember looking at the leader board and thinking, Would you guys just go away? Gimme a break!

When I came to number 17, the great par 3 that's set against the ocean and has all that history from U.S. Opens, like Nicklaus hitting the pin with a one-iron in the fog in 1972, and Watson chipping in from the furry rough on the back left to edge Big Jack ten years later, I had a two-shot lead. The pin was cut in the back left, which brings in all the trouble, but the tee wasn't all the way back. I felt if I could make a good swing there the tournament would be mine, and I just pured a six-iron in there about 12 feet from the hole. As I walked to the green, I thought, That shot just won it for me. Although I didn't make the putt, Duval also made par so I still had the two-shot lead going to the 18th, which is probably the most famous and photographed golf hole in the world.

Suddenly, I got very nervous. There are about six thousand miles of Pacific Ocean to the left, and out of bounds right, and a two-shot lead can evaporate instantly if you're not careful. Well, just as I was over my tee shot and getting ready to draw the club back, a lone seagull flew in front of me, about 80 yards out, and circled twice slowly. I thought, Why the hell is that seagull there to distract me? And then it popped into my head that it was my dad, telling me, "Hey, everything is fine. You are doing fantastic. Just rip this drive the way you have all day and finish this thing off."

I felt a great sense of calm come over me, and all of a sudden my mind was uncluttered and I ripped it right at the trademark tree in the middle of the fairway. I went on to birdie the hole, for a final round of 65, and Duval birdied it, too, to finish solo second. And then Jan rushed out and my brother David and my son Mick, who were watching that week, came out, and it was just a cloud-nine experience. I had hit all eighteen greens in regulation that day, and I believe sixty-nine of seventy-two for the week. I played the last thirty-six holes at my favorite course in the world in 13 under par. It was all I could do to hold in the tears when Clint Eastwood handed me the trophy.

As I was walking to the green on 18, I stared into the camera and said, "Lem, this one is for you. Next year we're finally going to make the damn cut." And sure enough, just as I was leaving the course that day, I got a call from him. And Jack had seen me play the last hole and heard my comment, and he told me how proud he was of me. To this day, it's the most elated I've ever been on a golf course.

The feelings of confidence and elation carried over to the next week when I won again at San Diego, by four shots, and again nearly every aspect of my play felt effortless. My work with Jim Hardy had put my golf swing on plane, and the accumulated knowledge over the years from instructors like Chuck Hogan and John Rhodes and Randy Henry was reaping the benefits. Through renewed desire, hard work, and finding a wonderful rhythm, I spent two charmed weeks in a great comfort zone.

In the next month, I had two more great chances to win, but fell just short at both Doral and Greensboro, losing by one stroke both times. At Greensboro, I hit a putt on the 17th hole that, if you watch the replay, seems to defy the laws of physics by not going in. The ball does a complete horseshoe around the cup, then spits in my eye. I get puckered even now thinking how that putt stayed out. They call golf a game of inches, but at times it's a game of millimeters.

For pretty much the first half of the 1995 season, I was able to stay in the zone, and during that four-month stretch I felt I was as good a player as anybody in the game. That makes it all the more remarkable to me that Nicklaus, for about twenty years, and Greg Norman for seven, and Tiger for the first eight years of his career, were able to stay at or near the top of their games and keep that passion and commitment to doing it right. It's just mind-boggling, because the commitments seem to increase exponentially the more success you have.

When I won those West Coast tournaments back-to-back, the offers to do radio shows and TV and print interviews increased fivefold, and my ex-assistant, Alana Snyder, had to take on another full-time intern to assist her in handling all the off-course opportunities and activities that came my way. Her own workweek went from forty hours to sixty during those summer and fall months. A local station in Portland even did a four-minute news feature on Alana, and how she scrambled during that time to keep up with all the requests. I think the people who booked the interviews saw that I had an open personality and a willingness to be outspoken about my profession, and I ended up saying yes to nearly everything that was thrown my way. I recognized that I was not going to stay in this zone for a whole lot longer, so I decided to enjoy my proverbial "fifteen minutes of fame" while it lasted. But suddenly I found that every fifteen-minute interview turned into a half hour, and before I knew it I was deluged. Some of it was really enjoyable, like an invitation to appear on *The Tonight Show with Jay Leno,* which I'll get to in a minute, but you have to be incredibly focused and disciplined and learn to say no or you'll quickly see your golf game become as fickle as the only woman on an island of shipwrecked sailors.

I'll never forget when Greg Norman was rising to the top and getting all that newfound attention, and then later when Tiger first turned pro. I talked to them both about how to schedule an hour for the media on Tuesday, and how to let the press know that you'll answer all their questions at that time. If a top player doesn't have a policy like that, he'll soon find that he's getting dozens of requests for that "quick five minutes," and his practice time will erode. You need to learn how to say *no* with a smile.

Whether you're playing in St. Louis, Pittsburgh, Philadelphia, or Miami, if you shoot 65 in the first round and are leading the tournament, there will be two hundred reporters looking for that fresh angle or hot scoop on the story of the day, and if you give everyone five minutes, the two hours you would spend on the range or in the fitness trailer is gone. So you then shoot 75 the next day, barely make the cut, and all of a sudden nobody knows your name. To stay on top for any period of time on the PGA Tour requires tremendous discipline, a backbone of steel, and the willingness to prioritize your time meticulously so that you keep your commitments to your family, your business, your mind and body, and your golf game. That is a really, really tough thing to do, and that is why I'm so impressed by guys who find a way to stay on or near the top year after year.

I recall Freddie Couples suggesting in a couple of interviews in 1992, after he'd won the Masters and risen to the stature of the best player in the world, that he wasn't certain he wanted all the responsibility and demands on his time that the number-one position required. Then, when Nick Price spent about three seasons as the top player right after Freddie, he felt the strong tug of his family and his native home in Zimbabwe pulling him away from the demands of the Tour. While both Couples and Price are still world-class players, I don't think either one of them greatly yearns to return to the very top of the sport again. The balance they've found in their lives between golf and family is a privilege they are not ready to sacrifice.

The candle burns out more quickly for some than for others. For me, after just four months at the very top of my game in May '95, and leading the PGA Tour in earnings, I was pretty exhausted.

A highlight of my brief time in the glare, as I said, was an invitation to appear on *The Tonight Show.* NBC was broadcasting the U.S. Open for the first time that year and the network was looking to give the Tour some late-night exposure. I was the leading money winner for the season at that point, so I got the nod. Other guests on the show that night were Jennifer Aniston, who was starring in the first season of *Friends,* and Kareem Abdul-Jabbar. It turned out to be a fun afternoon. I took Jan and her sister Jill with me to the NBC Studios in Burbank. We arrived a good two hours before the scheduled shooting time, which was five-thirty.

Jay Leno is a very cool guy. Although he doesn't know squat about golf, and I'm sure didn't have a clue who I was when I was booked, he made me feel like one of the major celebrities he's used to interviewing. When Jay saw that we'd arrived early, he invited the three of us down to watch as they went over final plans for the show. He even asked my opinion about one of the skits they were planning to do, and I was flattered to have my own dressing room, with my name on the door.

At one point I talked with his band leader, Kevin Eubanks, and I told Kevin that I played guitar and he asked if I wanted to sit in on one of the sets. I said, "No, no." For one of the few times in my life, I used common sense and didn't jump into the breach. It would have been like the club champion of Frog Bottom Muni teeing it up in the U.S. Open—way out of my league. All in all, Jay and his staff couldn't have been more accommodating. I thought: If this is how they treat some rummy golf pro, imagine what they do for somebody like Tom Hanks or Julia Roberts.

Anyway, once the show started and I was being interviewed, they did a preplanned skit. A golf ball came bouncing out on the set, you heard someone yell "Fore!" and then out came Jack Lemmon looking for it like it was one of his over-the-bluff bombs at Cypress Point. Jack saw us and feigned surprise, shouting, "Oh my gosh! Jay Leno! . . . Peter Jacobsen! . . . What are you guys doing here?" Of course, the audience went nuts, and with Lem on the set, the banter went smoothly and we had a great time.

Jay had admitted to me beforehand that his questions might not be of *60 Minutes* caliber, and I totally stumped him one time. He asked me something about the U.S. Open coming up soon, and then he fired one off the wall: He said, "Why do golfers all wear such crazy clothes, like orange pants and pink polka-dot shirts?"

I said, "Most guys don't really dress like that, Jay. But we do have one guy, Payne Stewart, who wears some pretty wild colors out there. He looks like the NBC peacock."

I was thinking that I was getting in a pretty good jab at my friend Payne, but Jay suddenly got this blank look on his face. It was obvious he didn't know who the hell Payne was, so it left him without a glib follow-up question. And then during the break, the producers warned me not to deviate from the script outline, because Jay didn't know much about the world of golf. If the names that Lemmon and I mentioned weren't Palmer or Nicklaus, we would lose Jay completely.

In another part of the show, they'd also been planning to throw a basketball to Kareem and ask him to spin it, but he wasn't interested. He actually told them he couldn't spin a ball, but I think what he meant was that he "wouldn't" spin one. I guess he thought it was a hokey idea, like asking me if I could make a two-foot putt. But I told them I could spin one, and so here I was on *The Tonight Show,* not hitting wedge shots or drivers, but spinning a basketball on my finger. The whole evening was a blast, and just one more novel experience golf has allowed me to enjoy before they finally plant me under the big divot.

I knew this might be a one-time experience. No matter how long you're in or near the winner's circle, there is an inevitable recoil. Your adrenaline level wanes, whether from lack of energy, lack of commitment, desire to experience other things in life, family obligations, or whatever. You get lazy and stop working and want to take a breather and enjoy the view when you get to the top of the mountain.

I wish there were a way for professional golfers to take a year off at some point in their careers to get that perspective, but it doesn't work that way. When you look at the life of a movie star, they can do a picture every two years, work their tail off while they're on a film, and then recharge their battery in between pictures—and they have a guaranteed salary. Professional baseball players, again, have the guaranteed contract and at least four months off between seasons, and they are protected and somewhat insulated on their teams. They come to the games in a team bus, enter the stadium through a roped-off area, and enter a locker room that is restricted before games to team personnel.

Other than the four hours we're in competition, professional golfers touch the public nearly every minute we're on the grounds. We park in the parking lot and sign autographs as we walk to the locker room. In the press room, we sign autographs and give interviews. In the locker room, we not only sign autographs but get interview requests. Anyone with a little juice with the tournament committee can get into our locker rooms on Tour, including a lot of the amateur players. For years, I've argued without success that the locker room should be off-limits to the media. Why do we have a press room if the locker room and the parking lot also qualify as media areas?

Even the practice area is fair game for media and autograph-seekers. I don't believe you'd ever see a fan allowed on the court for autographs while LeBron James is taking jump shots before an NBA game, or running to the 30-yard line as Peyton Manning is taking some warm-up throws, or standing in the on-deck circle as

Barry Bonds takes batting practice. Why should it be any different for the highest level of our sport?

I think the way Tiger handles all the attention and requests is by zoning out and going into his own little world. I have walked by him in the locker room and mumbled a greeting like "Hey, Tiger, how's it going?" and he walks right by me with his eyes focused straight ahead or down at the ground and he doesn't say a word. Now, Tiger is not a rude person or the kind of guy just to blow off another player. I think he's so in a zone he doesn't even hear you. I think he puts himself in that zone because he needs to be alone with his thoughts, to get totally prepared mentally for his round.

When a person is in that kind of fish bowl, like a Michael Jordan or Shaquille O'Neal, there's a need to find private time away from the crush, or the person will go crazy. About the only place that Tiger, or any one of us for that matter, can find sanctuary around the course is to go into the shitter and lock the door. I'll confess I've done that many times when I felt desperately in need of private, alone time with my thoughts. I might sit on the crapper and not even pull down my pants, just lean back and know that for a few brief moments it's highly unlikely that I'm going to be joined by someone from the *Orange County Register* or the *Las Vegas Review-Journal*, saying that he has just two quick questions and it won't take but a minute. I even have this hand-fart toy that I use at times like that, and I figure for every time I squeeze off that hand-fart, I buy at least another forty-five seconds of privacy. Even sportswriters are bright enough to understand that if a guy's eaten a bad burrito or some extra-strength chili, he needs to be left alone for a few minutes.

That brings up another major challenge that confronts us every day as professional golfers, and that is how to find a balance between family life and career. In 1995 I faced a number of questions when I elected to skip the Bob Hope Chrysler Classic. People just could not understand how I'd skip one of my favorite events, a tournament I'd won before, and return to Portland. How could I not try for the hat trick? the press wondered, and some of the commentators and columnists were critical of my decision. I was sort of tongue-tied in response because I couldn't come right out and say that I was planning that surprise fortieth birthday party for Jan that I described earlier. It's tough enough throwing a surprise party without dozens of reporters snooping into your private business. I never had even a moment's hesitation, though, that I was making the right decision.

I've always looked to guys like Nicklaus and Gary Player and Johnny Miller for advice not only about my profession, but also on matters of the family. Player and Miller each have six children and Nicklaus five, and those men have maintained close family ties in spite of spending more than 50 percent of their lives on the road. You have to wear a lot of hats in our profession and learn to be a lot of things to a lot of people. Those guys have always been loving fathers to their children, good husbands and supporters to their wives, courteous and considerate professionals to the golfing public and media, and friends and advocates for their fellow players.

I've had many more conversations with Player and Miller about family matters, and situations and challenges with our children, than I have about golf. I'm always interested in hearing how they handled parental responsibilities, because they've raised great kids, and that's every bit as impressive to me as their golf heroics. I am never going to reach their status with my golf accomplishments, but I hope I can show the same level of commitment and dedication to my family. It gets awfully tricky sometimes, though, balancing the home-and-away schedule.

I was at the birth of two of my children, but just missed being there when our first, Amy, was born. I was playing at Quad Cities, had made the cut, and called home to find out our baby was going to arrive earlier than expected. I withdrew, caught the first plane I could, but missed the actual delivery by twenty minutes. However, Jan got the nurses to let her keep Amy in her arms on the birthing table until I got there.

It also bothers me that I did not go along with Jan when Amy and Kristen went off to college—Amy to Syracuse University and Kristen to NYU. In both cases, I had committed to tournaments and wanted to withdraw, but Jan insisted I continue. As the bread-winner, it's always tough to balance whether I should play, because I might be going well and have a chance to make some serious money, or stop and do the family thing. I really don't think there is a hard-and-fast rule for what to do. It's a constant juggling routine.

5

Hartford in My Heart

I HAD BEEN PRACTICING that juggling routine for over twenty-five years when I arrived in Hartford for the Greater Hartford Open in late summer 2003. I thought I knew exactly what the future held for me—but, boy, was I wrong.

I've had a soft spot in my heart for Hartford, Connecticut, ever since I won the Sammy Davis, Jr., Greater Hartford Open in 1984 at the TPC of Connecticut (now known as the TPC at River Highlands). The current course is sort of a hybrid of old and new holes, since a redesign in 1990 by Roger Maltbie and Howard Twitty. The present course has had more cosmetic surgery than Michael Jackson, but it's a whole lot better-looking. I would now rate it one of the top Tournament Players Clubs in the country because it has a nice blend of hard and easy holes and requires a variety of shot-making skills. A lot of new courses, in my opinion—especially the ones designed by the big-name architects—are composed of virtually eighteen finishing holes. Playing them is like hitting yourself in the head with a hammer. It feels so good when you quit!

For some big-name architects, designing a golf course is an ego drill. Their goal is to build a tougher course than their contemporaries, so their plan goes something like this: Let's make number 1 a real bitch, then 2 will be a Frankenstein, 3 is going to scare the crap out of them, 4 will be a certified mo-fo, number 5 will really be a ballbuster, and 6 will be your basic frigging nightmare. And wait until they see number 7! As a player you're thinking, Great, so when do I get to make a par on this track? And amateur golfers can forget about it. They'd need an abacus to add up their scores.

When I entered the 2003 GHO, my thinking was that it could well be my swan song in Hartford, seeing as I would turn fifty in early '04 and spend the majority of my time on the Champions Tour. Even so, I certainly wasn't prepared for what happened on the Wednesday pro-am day preceding the tournament. I was paired with Chris Berman "the Boomer," an ESPN sportscaster and a good friend, but it rained all morning, so it was determined that the pro-am would be abbreviated to nine holes. When I got to the first tee, I noticed there was a bigger than normal crowd gathered around. Boomer was there, and so were Bill Murray and the tournament director, Dan Baker.

Boomer took a microphone and gave me a grand introduction and said that because this was my last tournament in Hartford, to commemorate my years of devotion to the event they had a special gift for me. Then Murray grabbed the mike and said, "Peter, I have known you for a long time and we've played a lot of golf together, and, boy, your turning fifty comes as a shock to all of us. Because quite honestly we thought you turned fifty about ten years ago." Then from an old black case he pulled a beat-up guitar that had been stepped through, its strings broken, its neck cracked.

"We know how much you love music," Murray said, "and so we thought we would give you a guitar that is commensurate with your musical ability. Enjoy."

I took the guitar from him while everyone was laughing, and

then Dan Baker came out and gave me a beautiful brand-new Ovation guitar. I was really touched by the gesture. I've made so many great friends in Hartford through the years and they were all there: tournament official Ted May and his wife, Debbie, and Peter and Jean Humphrey, and Dick Bruno. These are wonderful people and true friends. I found myself getting choked up, and even short of words, if you can believe that. And then after thanking everyone for their neat gift, I uttered something out of character. "As grateful as I am to everyone here," I jokingly said, "I don't want you to make too much of this being my last appearance here, because I'm going to win the tournament on Sunday, and I will be right back here next year as your defending champion."

We then played a nine-hole pro-am, and afterward conducted a clinic for the loyal fans who had braved the weather. At the clinic were former U.S. Open champion Scott Simpson, who is Murray's partner each year at Pebble Beach, and Boomer and Bill, and we all had microphones. I hit some shots, and then Scott hit a couple fades and hooks to demonstrate to the fans that it's possible to hit those kinds of shots intentionally, and then we got the gallery involved. A golf clinic is not like a movie, where no one is supposed to talk to the performers. If you go see *The Aviator,* and some guy from the audience is talking loudly to Leonardo DiCaprio up on the screen, you figure the guy is a psycho. At a golf clinic, we encourage psychotic behavior.

When some players do a clinic, they get very technical and try to give an intricate golf lesson. They'll talk about how many knuckles you should be able to see on your left hand at the top of the backswing or how much you rotate your right earlobe as you make contact with the ball or at what angle your left nostril is flared at impact. I'm not into that. I like a dash of instruction, maybe a sprinkle of psychology, and two tablespoons of entertainment.

When it was Murray's turn, he had a girl come out and hit some shots, and Bill of course made a mockery of the whole thing. Then he started scanning the crowd for another volunteer to come down, and he spotted a man who was about five-foot-ten and weighed at least 250 pounds. The guy's rather rotund shape wouldn't have been that noticeable had he not been wearing super-tight orange Dolphin running shorts that resembled a thong, and a white T-shirt three sizes too small. You've heard of those European swimsuits they call banana hammocks? This guy was wearing a sausage sleeve. There was a part of me hoping the man would come down and allow Murray to chastise him, and another part thinking, Stay where you are, pal. You don't need this humiliation. But when Bill implored the guy to come down, sure enough he did. Once we got a full body shot, we could see the rest of his ensemble included black knee-high socks and New Balance jogging shoes. The fashion critics on those cable shows could have spent an hour breaking down this guy's threads, and I tremble to think what the *Queer Eye* guys would have done to him.

Murray had a leery look on his face as he asked the guy to hit a five-iron shot, because he rightly sensed that this was the kind of dude who could have put a body slam on him if things got out of hand. But to my complete surprise, the guy ripped the iron shot about 180 yards right down the middle of the fairway. He then very stoically handed the club to Bill and walked back up the hill. After that mighty rip, his butt crack looked like it had totally devoured his shorts, and I remember getting this classic expression from Murray. It was like a memorable moment from *Saturday Night Live*. The visual required no commentary.

Anyway, I opened the GHO with a 63 on Thursday and either shared the lead or held it outright through the first fifty-four holes. On Sunday, I was paired with Chris Riley, one of my favorite young players on the Tour, and on that day he really showed some class. I'm convinced that as Riley's résumé fills up with victories, he's going to become one of the most popular players on Tour. Although Chris hit two balls out of bounds, including his opening tee shot, he hung in there and managed to finish solo second. And while the gallery was fully behind me and screaming my name coming down the stretch, he came over to me twice and remarked how cool it was to see the support they were giving me and how happy he was for me. As hard as he was trying to win himself, I know he actually meant it. To get that kind of response from a fellow competitor in the heat of battle is highly unusual.

There were all sorts of distractions during that final round, but over nearly thirty years of playing the Tour, I've learned how to turn potentially disruptive incidents into positives, and for me it's by confronting them head-on and trying to make them as fun as possible. It helps take the pressure off me.

At the Colonial National Invitational in 1984, I remember I was one stroke back of Payne Stewart playing the final hole, and I was paired with him. He hit his drive on 18 into the right hazard and had to take a drop. It was about a five- or ten-minute ruling, and I know the guys in the TV truck were thinking, C'mon, Payne, make par and don't drag this thing into a playoff, because the NBA Finals were about to start on CBS and a playoff would delay the start of the game—and in '84 we were talking the Celtics versus the Lakers, Bird versus Magic. So to kill some time, and with the cameras on me twiddling my thumbs in the middle of the fairway waiting for Payne's ruling, I started faking like I was dribbling a basketball, and I started backing into my caddie Fluff, hooking him with my arm and sticking my butt into him to get position as I went to the hoop. I was the poor-man's Kareem Abdul-Jabbar getting position on Robert "the Chief" Parrish in the post. It just seemed like something that the crowd would get a kick out of, and it in no way distracted Payne because he was so deep in the junk he couldn't even see me. And as I've said, that stuff helps reduce the pressure I'm feeling. As Trevino says, you only need about thirty to forty-five seconds to set up and execute a golf shot, and you have to do something to kill time in between and not get too caught up in the other stuff. And it worked out. I ended up beating Payne in a sudden-death playoff while basketball couch potatoes around the country cursed us for delaying their tip-off.

Back in Hartford, there was a guy doing motorcycle sprints beside the 14th tee—back and forth he'd go, as loud as a chain saw in your ear, and there was no way to ignore him, so I just waved to him and got a little interplay going and the gallery laughed at that. Then on the 15th hole, a great little risk-reward par 4 that can be driven from the tee but has water left, an extremely difficult pitching area to the right, and a severely sloped green, I hit a three-wood off the tee and missed the green to the right. The pin was in a front left position, and sloping nearly straight down toward the water from my ball. There was absolutely no way I could keep the ball on the green from where I was. It was a horrible pin placement, patently unfair for everyone, because the front left portion of the green on 15 is the precise area where all the players walk off to get to the 16th tee, so the ground is harder than a week-old pizza. Plus, I was on a downhill lie. If it were football I would have punted, in baseball I'd have called in a relief pitcher, in bridge I'd take a pass, but in golf I had to hit it. Naturally, all the fans around the 15th green who'd watched one ball after another roll off the green from my position were offering unsolicited advice.

"You've got to chip it," one man said.

"Hit a lob," whispered another.

I wondered out loud to my caddie, a fellow named Graeme Courts whom I'd borrowed from Loren Roberts for the week, whether I should even use a putter to bleed it down there.

"Don't putt it," said another voice.

So I'm getting all this "great taste, less filling" input, and I finally turned to the crowd and said, "Okay, what is it? Chip or putt?" Then I asked Graeme whether I was going to get penalized for seeking advice. All the dialogue just lightened up the crowd and relaxed me as well. I ended up hitting a pitch shot that rolled over the green, and while I was sizing up my third shot, Riley did something totally unexpected and pitched in for eagle. The game was definitely on again, but I was able to get it up and down for par and maintained a two-stroke edge.

Although I hadn't won on the PGA Tour in eight years, and certainly wasn't expected to win at age forty-nine, I felt calm all week. I had put together back-to-back-top tens not long before at Houston and Harbour Town, and didn't feel a bit uneasy coming down the stretch. On a 1-to-10 scale of nerves, with 1 being so calm I could fall asleep, and 10 being so nervous I couldn't trust a fart, I would have been about a 6—very in tune with what was happening, excited to be there, but with no fear or negative thoughts. On Tour, you don't really think so much about age. That is why a twenty-year-old Tiger Woods can kick a forty-year-old's ass, and vice versa. Craig Stadler won the B.C. Open at age fifty the same month I was in Hartford, and Jay Haas has been racking up top-tens and great finishes at age fifty and fifty-one, and I guarantee that when those guys are in the heat of battle they feel as fresh and vibrant and excited as when they were twenty-five or thirty. The game isn't that physically taxing, and I often think that experience and savvy can trump youth and agility in our sport. So the only thing I was thinking coming to the last couple of holes was that I was swinging well, the putter felt light in my hands, and there was no reason I couldn't close the deal.

As we left the 16th green, I had a two-shot lead over Chris Riley, and the same over Kenny Perry up ahead, and the crowd was totally behind me. They were yelling things like "You can do it, Jake!" and "Hang in there, Peter." Walking off the green, Chris came over to me and said, "This is awesome, Jake. Listen to that yelling. This is just awesome." Here was a young player in his twenties who understood that the better we make it for one another on Tour, the better we make it for all the players collectively. I thanked him for his comment, and I will never forget that he had the perspective to understand the situation and say that to me at a time when he was also trying to win.

The 17th hole at Hartford is a tough driving hole with water clearly in play off the tee, and we both hit solid three-woods down there. Mine went about 30 yards past where I expected it to be . . . adrenaline will do that for you. Chris hit a nice wedge in there about 8 feet away, and I threw a sand wedge that landed about 15 feet past the hole and sucked back to three feet away. When he missed and I made mine, my lead was 3 and I started to think I could enjoy one of those rare ceremonial walks up the 18th fairway. However, as I was walking to the 18th tee, my twenty-one-year-old daughter Kristen, who was a senior pre-med student studying neuroscience at NYU at the time and who had bought a Greyhound bus ticket to make the three-hour trip from New York with a friend to watch the final round, got through the ropes and couldn't contain herself. She wrapped herself around my shoulders and said, "Dad, you're going to win. You're three ahead with one hole to play." Kristen had never been present to see me win a PGA Tour event, and she was just ecstatic.

I certainly felt her joy, but I also knew the dangers of an early celebration. Matt Griesser, my partner on the Golf Channel, was with her, and I said, mainly for Matt's benefit, "Kristen, have you ever heard of Jean Van de Velde?"

She said, "Who?"

She doesn't follow golf that closely, but hard-core golf fans know the reference. Frenchman Jean Van de Velde came to the last hole of the British Open at Carnoustie in 1999 with a three-stroke lead, and a combination of questionable decisions and weird breaks led to his making a triple-bogey 8, and he lost in a playoff. I certainly didn't think that was going to happen to me, but in golf anything is possible.

I told Kristen to let me go ahead and par the final hole, and then we'd convene on the green.

I was able to do just that, and was delighted that Chris Riley birdied the final hole to finish solo second and make a tidy little sum of $432,000. My check for $720,000 was the biggest of my career and exactly ten times the amount I had won for my victory at Hartford nineteen years before.

After I holed the final putt, I hugged my caddie, hugged Chris Riley for being such a great sport, and then I was almost knocked off my feet by Kristen, who came charging onto the green and jumped on me. I felt like Brett Favre being sacked by Jevon "the Freak" Kearse on an option pass. She was so excited she came about three feet off the ground, and believe me when I say having my daughter there for that moment, with all those great Hartford fans so solidly behind me, is a moment that neither she nor I will ever forget. It made the victory doubly special.

When Dan Baker presented me with the winner's check, he reminded me of my prediction before the Wednesday pro-am. I'd actually forgotten that I'd boldly forecast the win. And when Dan heard the story of Kristen and her friend taking the Greyhound from New York for the day, he said, "Peter, we always provide a limousine to take the winner back to his hotel after the final round, but today that limo will be taking your daughter and her friend back to New York."

It was a terrific gesture, and the kind of special touch that makes a tournament like the Greater Hartford Open so special.

At the end of the 2003 season, primarily because of the win at Hartford, I was named by my peers as the PGA Tour Comeback Player of the Year. My final year-end winnings of $1,162,726 was the most I'd ever won in a season, after twenty-seven years, and at the age of forty-nine.

I thank Tiger Woods, television, the corporate sponsors, and the fans for the way the prize money has risen. In what other sport can you have your all-time *ka-ching* at that age? Maybe lawn bowling, but I doubt it.

6

Please . . . I'm Trying to Concentrate Here

My Hartford win was a surprise—but when you come right down to it, my favorite moments on a golf course occur when something totally unexpected happens to break the routine of the day. I'm not talking about holing a bunker shot or making a 50-foot putt with a triple break to save par. I mean the stuff that happens out of the blue and makes you realize that golf is just a game, and sort of a ridiculous game at that.

I'll never forget an incident that occurred in 1982 at the Danny Thomas Memphis Classic. It was a Wednesday morning pro-am, with a seven-thirty A.M. tee time, and I was in a salty mood. Just the day before I had missed qualifying for the U.S. Open at Pebble Beach by one stroke over thirty-six holes. I had been really counting on playing in the Open because, as you probably know by now, Pebble is my favorite course on earth. So about the last thing I was in the mood to do was act jovial and gracious to four strangers bright and early the next morning, but I was determined to try my best, because these guys had paid good money to participate and that's part of my responsibility as a professional golfer.

One of my amateurs was a big fellow, about six-foot-five and 250 pounds, with small feet and a high, squeaky voice with a buttery Southern accent. His name was Henry Brenner, and I didn't know quite what to make of him. With those tiny feet attached to that big body, I wanted to call him Twinkle Toes. On the first hole, Henry's tee shot went about 150 yards out and 250 yards to the right, deep into the wasteland. I immediately wanted to invoke the FIDO rule, which in layman's terms means, F—— It, Drive On. It's also called the No-Hunt rule because who the hell wants to find a ball that's been mistreated so badly and is en route to making an 11?

We got through three holes without anyone getting injured, but I was dragging and Mike Cowan was dragging even worse. Like me, Fluff was bummed that we'd missed the Open qualifying and he wasn't in the mood to yuck it up with my four new best friends. On the 4th hole, Henry excused himself, said he was hungry, and asked me if I wanted a Pronto Pup. I didn't know what he was talking about, but in about three minutes he came sauntering back with three foot-long corn dogs propped between his fingers. Now these babies were 12 inches long, deep-fried and certified artery-cloggers.

"Are you going to eat all of those?" I said.

"Oh, man," Henry said, all excited. "Let me tell you. I first played in this pro-am about four years ago with Nick Price, and I ate six Pronto Pups. The next year I played with Johnny Miller and I had eight. The next year I wanted to break my record so I had nine. And then last year, I had fourteen of 'em, but the last five didn't count because I hurled them on the way to the car. So today, I'm going for fifteen!"

After I heard that touching story, I decided I had to have a Pronto Pup, so I scarfed one and so did Fluff. And I think it gave him indigestion, because on the 5th hole we had a slight holdup and he said, "Peter, I need to make a pit stop. I'll be right back." And he snuck off into the trees beside the 5th fairway to do who knows what.

Mike was gone a few minutes, and Henry, burping cornbread and wiener, came over and said, "Peter, where's Mike?"

And I said, "He's taking a leak."

"Damn, he's in there about one hundred yards. Is he that modest?" Henry said.

I had my suspicions, but I just explained that Mike had had a long day on Tuesday with the Open qualifier and was trying to relax a little.

Henry picked up on the Cheech and Chong implication, and he thought that was funnier than hell. He said, "Let's have a little fun with ol' Fluff." He pulled out a big shiny badge and said, "I'm a reserve police officer in the Shelby County Sheriff's Department here in Tennessee, and I think we can pucker your boy up a little."

So Fluff came back a moment later, feeling far mellower, and Henry walked right up to him and said, "Hey, Fluff, Peter says I need to slow my swing down. I'm not hitting it too good."

Mike said, "What?"

Henry said, "Yeah, Peter says you've got something that will help me slow my swing down." Then he whipped out his badge, and with a dead-eyed look said, "Mike, you and I are going to have a little talk on the next tee about what's going on. I think there's something fishy here."

Mike's eyes bugged out of his head when Henry said that, and as soon as he walked over to hit his shot, Mike jogged off into the trees again, and he was eating cigarettes and throwing stuff on the ground and stomping on it, doing whatever he could to destroy the evidence. When he returned, he was as out of breath as the first guy to flunk out of Sherpa school.

We got to the next tee and Henry gave Mike an elbow in the

ribs. He said, "Ah, I'm just messing with you, Mike. I'm really just a stockbroker."

Henry and I both busted up, thinking how funny it was. But Mike was pissed the rest of the day . . . mainly because he had destroyed his attitude adjusters.

As long as I'm picking on Mike Cowan, I should mention the time I nearly killed him. I was playing in the Scottish Open at Gleneagles, which was a qualifier for the British Open if you placed in the top ten. In the third round I was on the edge of the green in two on the 6th hole, a par 5, and Mike had to relieve himself. Unlike at Memphis, he really did have to go this time, and there was only about one growler on the whole course, so I understood. There was a steep embankment to the left of the green, and Mike asked if I had gotten a good read on the putt, and I told him that I was all set, to go ahead.

I ended up leaving the long putt 5 feet short, and wanted his thoughts on the second putt, but it seemed like he was taking forever. When I didn't see his head coming over the rise, I figured he must be taking a dump, and I was hoping he wouldn't use our towel because we had twelve holes left to play. I hit a good putt on the 5-footer, but it did a full horseshoe lip-out and hung on the edge, so I was a little roasted. When I looked over to Mike for sympathy, he still hadn't reappeared. Now I'm thinking he might have the turkey trots or need a laxative, because the twenty-four-second clock on a good piss had gone off long ago. I walked off the side of the green and, half in frustration, flipped my putter over to my bag. Sure enough, the minute I released it, I sensed that I had a little too much gusto on it and I had a bad feeling. Just then, I saw the top of Fluff's head come over the bank. His head was down and he was fiddling with his zipper, but it was like he had a bull's-eye on his forehead. The putter head was going right for him. I yelled, "Mike, look out!" but it was too late. It caught him square above the eye and he went down faster than a Krispy Kreme doughnut at a Weight Watchers reunion. He lay there groaning. I didn't know whether to help him up or give him the mandatory eight-count. Actually, I wasn't laughing at all. I felt about two inches high. But darned if Fluff didn't rally and actually finish the round. A lesser man surely would have made me pack my own bag the rest of the way.

The next week, when we were playing in the British Open, Nick Faldo's caddie Fanne Sunneson asked Mike what had happened, how the entire left side of his face had turned into a boiled cabbage, and he was classy enough to say, "Ah, I whacked it in a door." I felt bad that he'd tried to cover for me, though, so I fessed up and told her I'd thrown a putter in his eye.

Fanne got this sad look in her own eye and said, "Aw, and I thought you guys got along so well."

ALL OF US WHO LOVE THE GAME of golf know that there's no better place to be than on a golf course with good company, especially when you're playing well. This next story speaks volumes about how fanatical golfers can be about their games.

In the fall of 2003, I was playing a casual round at The Bridges in Rancho Santa Fe, California, the site of the recent Battle at The Bridges. I was with Mike O'Connell; his brother Chris, a golf instructor who sometimes caddies for me; the course developer, Tom Martin; and Tom's cousin Darrell Wright. Now, Darrell was in his sixties and a pretty good golfer, and on that day he had a heckuva round going. He was about a 12 handicap, and through the first dozen holes he was only a few over par. He was playing his tail off and couldn't wait to tell his regular foursome how he hung right in there with a bunch of pros. The 13th tee overlooks the entire Santa Fe Valley and it's a breathtaking view. It was about two o'clock in the afternoon of a typically perfect Southern California day, and we were all having a ball. We hit our drives off the tee, and Chris, who is an athletic kid in his late twenties, jumped from the back tee to the men's tee, which is a drop of about 4 feet. And Darrell, who was loving life at that moment, decided to follow him, but when he jumped he caught his shoe on a rock edge. My back was turned, but I heard a loud pop, which was Darrell's leg snapping, followed by the most blood-curdling scream I've ever heard. I looked back and there was poor Darrell writhing on the ground and flapping his arms around like a cockroach that has been tipped on its back. His ankle was up in the air and bent at a grotesque angle. It was obviously a bad fracture, and the poor guy was in trauma. His great day of golf had turned into a nightmare in two seconds.

After a few moments, during which Darrell emitted only screams and gurgling sounds, we were able to roll him over and get him on his hands and knees, which was the first step in trying to get him to the cart so we could drive to the clubhouse and call an ambulance.

We eventually got our shoulders under his arms and held him so he could hop on one leg over to the cart. Each hop elicited a single guttural gasp. Darrell was keeping his broken leg elevated, and when we got to the cart he accidentally put his bad foot down and went, "Oh . . . oh . . . oh." And then he stopped dead cold and got this odd look on his face. And he set his bad leg down again, and then the blubbering and hyperventilating stopped completely. I was on Darrell's left side and he pushed me away suddenly and went into a mock golf stance. He suddenly looked up and said, "You know, it's not that bad. I think I can finish! I can hit seven-irons all the way in to the clubhouse."

We told him he was crazy, that we were heading to the club-house so we could rush him to a hospital, but he started begging us to let him finish. He insisted it was just a sprain and that he was sure he could go on. In ten seconds he had gone from wanting his leg amputated to thinking he could finish the round.

When we eventually got him to the hospital, he had a broken tibia and was on the shelf for a couple months. But just watching this man pleading with us to let him finish his dream round when his leg looked like the letter "L" told us Darrell was a true golfer, in every sense of the word. Damn, I had to admire his passion for the game.

REMEMBER MY STORY about John Daly at the Fred Meyer Challenge? Here's an even better one. A few years ago, Chuck "the Hit Man" Hiter was doing the clinic at the Challenge, and he elected to use two of the immortals in the game in one of his stunts. Chuck is an incredible talent, and he performs unusual golf feats that defy belief, like balancing on a basketball as he performs trick shots, and other stunts that require amazing strength and hand-eye coordination. Many of the Hit Man's stunts involve his taking a baseball swing at a moving ball with a golf club and making unbelievable contact. (If you don't think that's tough, just throw a golf ball in the air and take a rip at it with a driver. I'll give you 10 to 1 you whiff it cold.) He has one trick in which he drops a golf ball down a huge flexible tube, about 15 feet long and shaped like a J, then sprints to the other end of the tube, and as the ball comes flying out he rips it down the fairway with a driver. The stunt requires two volunteers to assist him: a person to hold one end of the tube over his head, and another to kneel down and hold the bottom end of the tube where the ball comes shooting out a millisecond before the Hit Man blasts it. So we were there with all the pros and celebrities and grandstands full of fans, and who do you suppose Hiter pulled up to assist him but Jack Nicklaus and Arnold Palmer.

Chuck asked Jack to hold the high end over his head, looking like the Statue of Liberty, and he had Arnold get down on one knee and hold the bottom end. Arnold didn't quite get what was happening, and he was looking around like, What the hell am I doing here? But he was going to be a good sport and go along with the act.

Chuck dropped a ball in the high end and went sprinting around to the lower end, where Arnie was kneeling sort of nonchalantly, like a quarterback in a sandlot game drawing a play in the dirt. As the ball came shooting out about a foot in front of Arnold's face, the Hit Man took a huge Sammy Sosa swipe and the ball came off the toe of the club and it was louder than hell. Palmer's eyes popped out of his head like somebody had just clipped off a testicle. He needed an instant change of underwear. And then, because the Hit Man hadn't caught it flush, he did it again. Arnold looked like he had seen a ghost. And Jack said, "Damn, I'm glad I'm holding the high end!"

After the clinic was over, I said to Chuck, "What were you thinking, Chuck? You could have killed Arnie!"

He said, "Yeah, I could have. But I just looked into the audience and saw the two most famous men in golf, and I thought, How cool if I could put them in the show!"

As long as I live, I'll never forget the look on Arnold's face. It's probably the only time in his life that he's been scared shitless.

7

A Senior Moment . . . Interrupted

I T WAS THE THOUGHT of joining people like Jack and Arnie that really had me going as I crossed into the year 2004. Some wise guy once said, "I've waited my whole life to turn fifty." Well, that's the feeling you have as a touring professional when the Champions Tour is waiting for you. Each event is typically fifty-four holes, there's no thirty-six-hole cut to worry about, the fields are limited, and you're guaranteed a paycheck.

There's no other sport that offers players a chance to actually increase their income after the age of fifty. When you consider that athletes in the four major sports are generally considered well over the hill at forty, we golfers have to be damn grateful for the opportunities we have as "seniors" to still get that competitive rush of trying to win golf tournaments and at the same time make great money. Guys like Jim Colbert, Bruce Fleisher, Jim Thorpe, and Dana Quigley have made far more money on the Champions Tour than they did in their primes. In fact guys like Quigley and Allen Doyle were barely known outside their home states until they qualified for the senior circuit, where they became bona fide stars.

As I was going through a couple of lean years between 2000 and 2002, and undergoing hip surgery in May 2001 that kept me out of action for four months, my thinking was that when I turned fifty in March 2004 I would charge onto the Champions Tour and play nearly every week. However, I threw myself a career curve ball when I won the Greater Hartford Open. That victory gave me another two and a half years of full exemption on the PGA Tour, and the luxury of being able to pick and choose between regular Tour events and Champions Tour events through the end of the 2005 season.

I also knew as I approached fifty that I wasn't ready to quit playing in my favorite Tour events, such as the AT&T and the Hope and the Colonial and Jack Nicklaus's Memorial at Muirfield Village. I have so many good friends at those places, and those tournaments are such special events, that I hope to play in them several more times, as long as I'm either eligible or welcome.

But then there was the part of me anxious to get back and hang out with old friends on the Champions Tour, guys like Hale Irwin and D. A. Weibring and Mark Lye. I used to have a locker next to Hale at most Tour events, because they are often done alphabetically, and Mark Lye, who is now a talented broadcaster on the Golf Channel, played rhythm guitar on our non–Grammy-winning band Jake Trout and the Flounders. So joining a Tour that allowed me to compete against and hang out with so many of my old friends was very appealing.

Turning fifty in professional golf instantly transforms you from being an old fogy in one context to the new kid on the block—in one day's time. On the Champions Tour, I would be joining not only my contemporaries, but also the guys I grew up emulating.

I get asked a lot why I don't mimic the swings of younger players like Tiger Woods and Phil Mickelson, and the reason is that I grew up admiring players like Lee Trevino and Gary Player and

Hubert Green and Johnny Miller. Those were the guys winning golf tournaments, or doing commercial endorsements on television, and they had the most easily identifiable swings. I could find the distinctive features in each one, and I'd practice them in the mirror as a kid, and then replicate them to make my mom and her friends laugh and show them how clever I could be. I guess I had a natural gift for mimicry because I learned them pretty quickly, along with those of contemporaries like Craig Stadler, Tom Kite, and Lanny Wadkins.

There's another reason I don't imitate Tiger's swing when I do exhibitions. I'm afraid I might hurt myself. I feel like I'm going to pull a groin muscle just watching those vicious swipes he takes when he's extricating a ball from deep rough.

Anyway, when I got to Valencia, California, for the SBC Classic in mid-March 2004, everyone was making a big deal of my senior debut, and I was welcomed warmly. I enjoyed seeing guys I hadn't talked to in a while, like John Jacobs, J. C. Snead, and Charles Coody, and my European friends like Sam Torrance and Mark James.

I have a good working relationship with the Golf Channel, through my television show *Plugged In* and other projects, and partly because of that, those guys really laid it on heavy during their telecast of the SBC Classic. They led into commercials with some of Jake Trout and the Flounders' "greatest hits"—if there is such a thing—and I had a camera in my face constantly as I walked down the fairways. Marketing campaigns on the Champions Tour always emphasize the guys who just became eligible, but they went so far with it at Valencia that I actually felt the need to apologize to announcer Tom Nettles on the air. I was concerned that viewers might get nauseous from overkill. But I can't deny that I had a super time all week and that it was flattering to get the attention. Without a doubt, my goal for the week was to win, but it was

equally important that I enjoy myself and try to add some entertainment value to the event.

While I didn't win, I stayed in the hunt the entire way. I opened
and closed the fifty-four-hole tournament with 67s, but I missed
some opportunities in the second round, when I shot 71. I finished
solo third and won $108,000. My 11-under-par total was three shots
behind winner Gil Morgan and one behind Larry Nelson. I
learned something I already suspected, and that is that these guys
had barely lost a step since they'd played on the PGA Tour. The
old line "If you couldn't beat us then, you won't be able to beat us
now" has a lot of truth to it.

I was asked afterward if finishing third at a Champions event
was as satisfying as placing fourteenth at the AT&T (the prize
money was about the same), and I really had to think about that
one. The truth is that the PGA Tour is and always will be the ultimate stage, so when you perform well there, it's a great feeling, especially after being on Tour as long as I have.

However, if I were asked to compare the "fun quotient" between that first Champions event and a regular tournament, there's
no comparison. I'd go with the old farts. I had an absolute blast
playing at Valencia. I was paired the first round with Don Pooley
and Wayne Levi, both good friends, and I was paired the next day
with Jose Maria Canizares, against whom I had competed in a Ryder Cup match in 1985. The last day, I drew Pooley, for the third
straight round, and Hale Irwin, whose record clearly shows him to
be the best Champions Tour player ever. A month later, he would
win the Senior PGA Championship, which marked his fortieth
win since he turned fifty. That's a high-water mark that may never
be reached again. There was a lot more casual conversation going
on in those rounds than in a typical PGA Tour event, and anyone
who knows me knows I'm not averse to a little chatter.

I had heard some rumbling from guys that I might not enjoy

the weekly requirement on the Champions Tour to play in two pro-ams preceding the tournament, but I didn't expect to have any problem with that. I have built my entire business career and my events-management company, PJP, in large part through making friends and business associates in pro-ams. On the Champions Tour, we play with four amateurs on Wednesday and four on Thursday. I do find it strange that the top players are required to play only in the Thursday pro-am. That seems backward to me. If I were making the rules, I would want to give the amateurs what they most desire, and that is to play with the top players, not the guys further down the money list.

I do find it refreshing that, in the last two years, the Champions Tour has become highly competitive. Last year there were twenty-two different winners, and in one stretch, seventeen different guys found the winner's circle in consecutive events. In 2004, ten different players won the first ten events. That's extremely healthy and provides competitive suspense that didn't exist in the Tour's early years. I can remember when Peter Thomson won nine events in 1985, Bruce Crampton won twelve tournaments in the next two seasons, Chi Chi won seven events in 1987, Trevino dominated in the early nineties, and then there came a time when it seemed as if every event was won by either Larry Nelson, Gil Morgan, or Hale Irwin. After that came a five-year stretch during which Irwin dominated like no one before. The Champions Tour became something of a victim of its own predictability.

While at the end of every season there are always players who stand out, the wealth is being shared much more equally now. The fact that so many tournaments are fought tooth and nail down to the last hole, with the outcome always in doubt, makes for good theater for golf fans and is healthy for our tour and our sponsors.

The decade between age forty and fifty used to be considered a "limbo" period for many players, when their earnings started to

dry up and they were inclined to find more outside sources of income until they reached the Champions Tour, but that is no longer
the case. In 2003, fifteen official events were won by players forty or
older, the most ever in PGA Tour history, and with Vijay Singh
winning nine events in 2004 after turning that corner, it appears
that life on Tour now "begins at forty." Purses have increased so
dramatically that if a player has enough game to finish in the top
125 on the money list, he's pretty much guaranteed to make at least
three-quarters of a million dollars in income, and that's hard to
match by giving lessons or endorsing aluminum ball retrievers.
Another reason for the change: Tour players now build fitness and
stretching exercises into their daily regimens because they want
their bodies to be able to stay competitive until they reach their
mid-sixties and beyond. Who can forget Nicklaus early in his
career saying that he couldn't imagine playing competitive golf
past the age of forty? But there he was in the middle of the 2004
season debating how much longer he wanted to compete . . . at age
sixty-four.

ANYWAY, THAT WAS MY PLAN: charge onto the Champions Tour,
pick my favorite PGA Tour events, have a blast. But the golf gods
don't care about plans.

Even though I'd had an encouraging start to the 2004 season,
with several solid finishes and my first seventeen rounds at even
par or better, there was a nagging concern in the back of my mind.
My left hip didn't feel good. I felt a lingering pain there when I hit
full shots. It was the same hip on which I'd had surgery in May
2001, but it was a slightly different pain. Because I was playing
well, I just tried to block it out and hoped that it would get better.

Then I got food poisoning at Bay Hill and had to withdraw,
which was a disappointment because I love Arnold's tournament

and hated not to be able to finish. The competitor in me always wants to finish any tournament I start, to gut it out no matter how bad I feel and post a score, but it's simply impossible to rip two-irons when you're feeling like Linda Blair with a stomach full of split-pea soup and the exorcist uttering incantations. Retching also doesn't play well on network television, unless you're in the second round of *Fear Factor*. I didn't want to end up on a highlight reel for Extreme Sports.

"And now, here's Peter Jacobsen. He's got 237, wind slightly hurting. He's chosen a two-iron. This ball needs to carry at least 225 to clear the hazard. He draws the club back, and . . . Oh my God. Thar she blows! His head is spinning on its axis. It's not pretty, sports fans. We can only wonder now whether the officials will lime off that area and give players a free drop from the . . . shall we say . . . not-so-casual water."

Even though I was still pretty weak from several days in bed, I drove to Jacksonville for The Players Championship. I hadn't been eligible to play in what is often called the "fifth major" in a couple of years, so I didn't want to miss the opportunity to compete on a great course against what is the best field in golf. I sucked it up and got gradually stronger as the week went along, and stood at even par after fifty-four holes. But then everything went to hell on Sunday. I didn't feel well, my hip was hurting more than ever, and on top of that I played like a dog. I posted a pretty little 83, with nine bogeys, a double, and no birdies. It was one of the worst rounds I've ever shot in my career.

I had a few weeks off before my next start, so I took care of a lot of business matters, and despite my hopes that the irritating pain in my hip would subside during the break, it didn't. After a first-round 73 at the MCI Heritage in mid-April, I withdrew. The very next day, I went to see the specialist who'd performed my first hip surgery, Dr. Marc Phillipon, and he scheduled me to go under the knife the following Tuesday, April 20. I've seen too many players put off decisions like that because they hope the problem will mend itself and they don't want to face the time off, and the result often is that they end up missing even more months of competition. I wanted to take my medicine and carry on.

From what Dr. Phillipon told me, the cartilage on the labrum in my hip had completely worn off, so he had to reattach cartilage at the very top of the hip. Surprisingly, this injury was not related to the hip operation I had had in '01. I saw X-rays from the earlier surgery and that repaired cartilage tear was holding up beautifully.

Soon after the second operation, the doctor told me it had gone well, but that I needed to be diligent through the physical rehabilitation process. We set a goal of my returning to competition by the middle of June.

One way to look at my predicament in April is to think of an ottoman with a slipcover. I'd actually torn about a third of the slipcover off the ottoman, so Dr. Phillipon had to go in and reattach it. He told me later that he'd had to drill into the bone a little bit to reattach the cartilage, and that bone pain is the worst pain you can have. George Thorogood and the Destroyers obviously knew what the doctor was talking about when they recorded their classic "Bad to the Bone."

I asked the doctor if something in my golf swing had caused the two injuries, and he said he didn't think so. He explained that some people are just susceptible to certain problems, in the same way that certain people are more prone to skin cancer than others, and some have more brittle bones.

The low point of the experience came the morning after surgery. I was kinda groggy and spaced out, so when I woke up I was just grateful that I wasn't walking toward the blinding light. The first face I saw was this rosy-cheeked Irishman named Kevin.

He was all bright and cheerful and said, "So how are ya this morning?"

And being in a dream state from the long surgery, my first thought was, Yeah, screw you, you giant leprechaun! Go jump in the clover. No one should be this happy this early. But I said, "Just fine, how are you?"

He said, "Great. Now let's get up on this bike and start working out that hip." I saw a stationary bike sitting in the room that hadn't been there the night before, and I assumed Kevin was kidding about my getting on it. The invitation was the equivalent of asking a man who's just had his legs amputated if he wants to go for a jog. But it was obvious after a few long seconds that Kevin wasn't kidding. There wasn't even a hint of a smile. A female nurse was there with him and she said, "Would you like a pain shot right now?"

I've always hated pain pills because I don't like being totally out of it. So I instinctively shifted into my John Wayne mode and said, "Nah, I'm fine."

Over the next five minutes, I struggled out of bed. And anything resembling modesty goes right out the window at moments like that. I was showing more skin than Paris Hilton on a Las Vegas weekend. I had that delicate little standard-issue nightie on, no undies, and an open vent in the back. You've heard of Plumber's Crack? I was showing San Andreas Fault. And as I was scooting out of bed, I didn't even care if the nurse could see Mr. Chubby. The only good thing was that I knew I wouldn't leave any skid marks on the sheets, because I was about six weeks away from a good bowel movement.

I was in such pain just trying to get vertical that strange noises were coming out of my throat. Eventually, Kevin helped me get up and he put a little footstool under my right leg. Then he slipped some crutches under my arms. He was such a nice guy; he was pulling my skirt down in the back like he was trying to protect my modesty.

Actually, once I was on my feet I started to feel a little better, but that was only momentary because I had to mount the bike. Obviously, getting on it like normal, tossing one leg over the bar and settling in, was an impossibility. I had to grab the handles and crutch up onto this other stool that was right next to the bike. Think of trying to prop a hundred-year-old man on a horse, and you'll have the picture.

My left leg was trailing behind me, like Igor in *Young Frankenstein,* and it felt like I was dragging a cement block. It took a full ten minutes to get situated on the bike and get my feet into the stirrups, and once I accomplished that I had to call for a time-out. My whole body was shaking and perspiration was dripping off me like I'd just finished grooving to Richard Simmons's *Sweatin' to the Oldies* tape. I felt about as stable on that immovable bike as though I'd hopped onto a unicycle for the first time.

So the nurse asked me again, "Are you sure you don't want a pain shot? You look like you could use one."

Like an absolute freakin' idiot, I said, "No, I'm fine, I'm fine." And I started to pedal, but try as I might I couldn't get that damn pedal to go 360 degrees around. So I just sort of rocked it back and forth like a Ferris wheel slowing to a stop, letting off one passenger at a time. My hip and leg hurt so bad I was nearly crying, but I was determined to get that thing to go around and start this agonizing rehabilitation process. For heaven's sake, I told myself, I'm a professional athlete. I can certainly pedal a damn stationary bike.

For the first couple of minutes the odometer registered zero miles per hour. I kept churning, though, and finally I made progress. Once I got it moving, I kept it going for about ten to twelve minutes. After what felt like an eternity, Kevin said, "Okay, that's enough for today. We'll get on it again tomorrow."

I dismounted, although "toppled off" is a more accurate description. I noticed that sweat drops were dripping down the pole of the bike. I had been bare-assed on the seat, and for the next rider the sight was not pretty. A bed has never looked as inviting as that hospital cot when I crawled back into it. It was like, Thank God, my work is done for the day. I can turn back into a human toadstool.

About ten minutes went by, and as I was catching my breath, the pain set in. And did it ever! It was intense. I asked Jan to get the nurse, and when she came in I explained that I was not in mere pain, but *severe* pain, mind-rattling pain, poked-in-the-eye-with-a-sharp-stick pain.

The nurse said, "I told you you needed a morphine shot before you got on that bike."

I said, "Okay, you were right. You were right. Give me a morphine shot."

She said, "No, I'll give you a Percoset."

I said, "Give me two. They're small." But she gave me just one.

So I ate it, and it didn't do squat. A couple of minutes later, she gave me another one. Nothing. It was like I'd eaten two cherry Skittles. Anyone on pain medication will tell you that you have to stay ahead of the pain, that it's tough to catch up to it once it has set in—and I was trailing this demon by a full lap. The pills had no effect whatsoever. Finally, Jan could see I was in the worst pain of my life. I'll admit that I was actually crying. Check that, I was sobbing. Yeah, I may have been the new kid on the Champions Tour, but I felt like the oldest, most broken-down organism on the planet.

It was the first time in my adult life I can recall crying from physical pain. I'm not certain that, had there been a gun handy, I might not have ended it right there. The pain was that bad. Like that young mountain climber who was trapped on the rock wall and cut his arm off, I would have just taken a chain saw and removed my leg at the hip. You know the old Coyote Ugly joke? I would have been Coyote Jake, the dude who chewed off his own leg.

My thought process when I'd refused the shot earlier was that I didn't want to be gooned up for fear of missing *Judge Judy* at eleven A.M. or a rerun of *Law & Order* on TNT, or maybe an old *Newlywed Game* with Bob Eubanks asking a couple about the most unusual place they'd ever made whoopee. The real truth is that I hate all forms of medication that take me out of the real world. But was I ever regretting my bravado! After about twenty minutes, the nurse finally got the requisition order for the morphine shot, and about three minutes later the God-sent narcotic kicked in. I could live again. But in a couple hours, I needed another one. The pattern never varied. I would nod off once the morphine set in, but then I would wake up itching. I was in Round Two of *Fear Factor,* where they unleash the cockroaches and black widows and lock the contestant in a mirrored coffin. I begged Jan to scratch my back and other important places, hard-to-reach places . . . places only your loved one would dare to go, and then only because she had taken a vow about sickness and health. As I lay in that hospital bed, I felt great empathy for a golfer like Casey Martin, and the pain that he has every day on the golf course, and for all the other people with disabilities who tough it out from one day to the next.

I even thought back to Hartford the previous summer, to winning a Tour event at age forty-nine for the first time in eight years, and having my daughter Kristen, who was just finishing her premed courses at New York University, rush onto the green and hug me. She was crying with happiness and excitement because she had never been present to see her dad win a tournament. If that day in Connecticut was a 10 on the "life's great moments" scale, I was now at a zero and heading into the black hole of minus 2. My schedule for morphine shots was every three hours, but after about two hours and forty-five minutes my hip would start twitching. Remember when Roy Rogers would ask Trigger how many people were trapped in the cave, and Trigger would paw the ground with his foreleg and count them out—one . . . two . . . three . . . four? That's what my leg was doing, as a way of signaling any hospital workers happening by my room that it was time for my shot. I was a full-fledged junkie within the first four injections.

I also rediscovered what true love is in that hospital bed. And no, it wasn't for Kevin, my cheerful rehab guy. As I said, as I was lying in bed I would get to itching so bad it was nearly unbearable, and Jan would scratch that puppy wherever it barked. But that wasn't the worst part. When I was up on that bike going through my requisite torture in the days following the surgery, I'd suddenly have to piss, but I couldn't move off that bike in near enough time to solve the problem. So I'd say, "Honey, could you reach down there and see if you can find Mr. Chubby? And if you'll be so kind, could you aim him into this plastic bottle here?"

And Jan would search around under my Victoria's Secret sanitary gown with an ungloved hand, looking for the Chubster, and just when the dam was about to burst she would locate him and guide him to the open spout. It was sort of like trying to find an old Milk Dud between the cushions of your grandmother's favorite couch. It required serious digging and a miner's lamp, but she would eventually hit pay dirt.

Of course the first three or four times she did this, the old boy wouldn't do what was required of him. All the muscles in that area had gone on full lockdown. Naturally, on those rare times when it did work, the damn bottle was too small. It held 20 ccs and I had stored up 80 ccs of orange juice and liquid morphine. The only thing more impossible than pedaling a bicycle the day after your hip has been surgically violated is turning off the spigot on a three-day piss buildup once the nozzle is wide open. I burned off more calories stopping the spigot than I did in a half hour on the bike.

The expected rehabilitation period for my recovery was six weeks, and the first four weeks I spent four to six hours a day sitting in a chair while a motorized rotation device worked the hip joint constantly. I slept in a regular bed but I had to wear a brace, which went from my waist all the way down to my foot and locked the leg in a position that didn't allow any clockwise rotation in the hip. I didn't ask a lot of questions of Dr. Phillipon when he issued instructions, because he is considered the foremost expert in the world at this surgery, and he has performed it on several other Tour players, like Greg Norman, Jesper Parnevik, and Steve Elkington.

The doctor did say that when the body gets older, extra weight gets put on the hips and knees and ankles, so that could have been part of my problem, but the main aggravation on those joints for a professional golfer comes from the repeated motion of turning around the hips hundreds of times a day, month after month, year after year. There's a lot of torque in the golf swing on the hips, knees, and ankles. It was interesting to observe how a specialist's mind works. After he'd made the diagnosis of the injury, Marc asked me whether I flared my left toe toward the target when I hit shots. And I said yes, because that's what Ben Hogan recommended in his classic instruction book *Five Lessons: The Modern Fundamentals of Golf.* Hogan said to aim your left toe out at a 45-degree angle, midway between the target and straight in front of you.

The doctor said, "I've found in my research that that angle is very detrimental to your hips." He explained that when a golfer opens his left foot, that allows the left leg to turn 180 degrees through the ball, which can hurt the hip joint because it starts putting pressure on the back side of the joint. He told me that when I started hitting balls again, he wanted me to square up my left foot, which would cause me to post up on my left side, preventing my left leg from turning too far. That would alleviate the wearing on the back of the hip joint. I called my teacher Jim Hardy, and he said we could work on that and it shouldn't be any big adjustment. He also suggested that now that I was over fifty, I was going to have to practice with a little more common sense. He wanted me to hit maybe only forty or fifty full shots on the range after a round, rather than pulling a Vijay Singh and hitting until the lights go down and the sprinklers come on. It's sort of like putting a pitch count on a veteran pitcher, knowing that his arm doesn't have quite the zip it did as a rookie. Professional golfers make adjustments all the time, and if these changes would keep me off that damn bike and away from the indecent exposure and the morphine, it was a change I was happy to make.

My mind went a lot of different places during my nearly two months of rehabilitation. I've always kept a more than full schedule and have questioned many times how I could handle the responsibilities of fatherhood, a competitive golf career, a television career, a management company, golf course architecture, an exhibition and corporate client schedule, and all these other things at once. And all I can say is that I enjoy all of it, and the variety keeps me motivated and fresh to do all the different tasks. I've never questioned it a bit, and feel grateful that I'm needed or wanted by that many people. So when I'm forced to stop cold turkey, as I was after the surgery, it's one of the few times I really have a chance to reflect on my life. And so I spent much of that recuperation time reflecting on how we all tend to take our health for granted, and how much I enjoy playing golf and competing at a high level.

THE TIME TO REFLECT reminded me of the year I spent in the broadcast booth for ABC, back in 1993. I'd been up there commentating and watching guys hit shots and face putts under pressure and thinking, Oh my God, I can't just sit here and watch this. It's driving me crazy. I want to be hitting the shots and let other guys do the describing. The result of the inactivity was that I found myself working hard on my game to get back to the field of battle, and then again after both my surgeries in '01 and '04, I worked harder on my rehab exercises, swimming, bike pedaling, and diet, whatever it took to bring the inactivity to an end. I am a good patient in terms of doing what the doctor tells me to, because that's all part of the rehab. I knew that I had to be diligent and disciplined if I wanted to continue to play at the highest level. Anything less, and there were another dozen guys itching to take my place.

Sooner or later, I knew, I was going to have to put it to the test.

8

The U.S. Senior Open:
How It All Went Down

To say that I had concerns about my chances going into the U.S. Senior Open at Bellerive Country Club in St. Louis in late July is well beyond an understatement. I had more question marks on my chest than Matthew Lesko—you know, that goofy guy in the infomercials who pitches government grants and screams at the camera?

I had played just five competitive rounds since April 15, a few days before I had my hip surgery. I'd recently played thirty-six holes as Chris Riley's partner in the CVS Charity Classic in Rhode Island, a great event hosted by Billy Andrade and Brad Faxon and managed by my company, PJP. It's a fun, relaxing best-ball tournament, and while I was pleased with the way I played, I knew that going more than two rounds would have been really tough. Although my swing felt great, the walking was no picnic. Hip surgery provides new meaning to Mark Twain's classic line that "golf is a good walk spoiled."

And although I had managed to finish all three rounds of the Commerce Bank Long Island Classic on the Champions Tour over the Fourth of July, my scores told the story of my condition: I had a great first round, shooting a 7-under-par 64, but then I literally and figuratively hobbled in with 74 and 71 on the weekend, tying for twenty-sixth. It was all I could do to finish the event. At the end, my hip was barking like a pit bull with an impacted wisdom tooth.

However, I was determined to tee it up again the following week. It was the second major of the year, the Ford Senior Players Championship, and during my recuperation I had already missed the first major, the Senior PGA Championship, which had been played the previous month. Although I'm not one to give undue importance to the Champions Tour majors, or put them on any kind of equal plane with the majors on the regular PGA Tour, nevertheless they are our biggest events and they determine who still has that great competitive fire and ability to beat the best fifty-plus golfers in the world when they are totally focused. And as a rookie hoping to make a big impact immediately in this new league, I had every hope prior to the season that I would be right in the thick of the battle in every major.

So we were playing the Wednesday pro-am prior to the Senior Players in Dearborn, Michigan, and I could make it through only thirteen holes before my hip seized up so bad I had to be taken off the course in a cart. I couldn't even walk in. At that point, I was zero for two in teeing it up in Champions Tour majors. The good news was that I had two weeks to go before the British Senior Open began, and that was a tournament I had been looking forward to for over a year.

I was taking the entire Jacobsen clan—Jan, Amy, Mick, and Kristen—plus my old caddie Fluff to loop for me. It was going to be a great family vacation, with a plan to check out all the fun spots around Portrush, Ireland. Fluff and I both love golf "across the pond," and we have many wonderful memories of the British

Open, not the least of which is that infamous streaker tackle in 1985. My only disappointment was that whole episode didn't elicit even one call from an NFL talent scout. And I know for a fact that there were several teams in the mid-1980s that were shallow at linebacker.

ON MONDAY OF THE SENIOR BRITISH, I played a practice round with Dana Quigley, Dale Douglass, and Bobby Lincoln, and felt great starting out, but early in the round it was clear to me that I couldn't make all eighteen. I played seven holes and told the guys to forgive me, but I had to jump over to the back nine because it was gonna be a short day. I played numbers 15 and 16, and then walked in. And this was only Monday. My hip problem was one that couldn't be ignored. It's very basic: if you can't walk, you can't play. The irritating thing was that my swing felt great, and with the help of my teacher Jim Hardy I had made posture adjustments that allowed me to make a good full turn without a hint of pain. However, walking between shots was killing me. The pain was sort of like doing bicep curls with a heavy weight: you do five repetitions, then six (it's starting to burn), seven (you barely get through it), and then all of the money in the world can't get you to do an eighth. Your arm just cramps and quits working. That's what would happen to my hip when I'd walk too far. All the muscles in my butt, left thigh, and calf would literally cramp up to the point where I couldn't take a normal step. However, if I lay down and rested for twenty minutes and did some leg stretches, I could start walking again. Even if I lay down on the green or tee and stretched for a ten-minute break, I was fine. But in a tournament round, you can't stop for twenty minutes. You've got to keep going, and that was my problem. I didn't want to be out there in a major championship doing a Jack La Lanne exercise routine on every tee.

Anyway, on Tuesday I played the pro-am with a fabulous group of Portrush members. They were wonderful chaps, fun and enthusiastic, and I was having a great time with them telling stories and enjoying the typical Irish day—it was windy and rainy, like that scene from *Caddyshack*. Again, however—this time after the 11th hole—I started to cramp up. I played the next four holes like my old partner Jack Lemmon—right . . . left . . . clank—and then realized I wasn't accomplishing anything that would help me during the tournament, so I had Fluff play the last two holes. It was a fun day, but it was quickly dawning on me that my hip was not going to let me go the distance, especially in the chilly Irish mist that was certain to continue through the week. I wasn't ready to raise the flag just yet, however.

I took Wednesday off and visited a physical therapist in Portrush named Adam Wilson. I rested and stretched and took hot baths. On Thursday I had an afternoon tee time, but I was still stiff and sore, and I realized I couldn't go. I didn't want to start the tournament knowing I couldn't make all seventy-two holes, and thereby take up a spot that an alternate could use. With regret, I phoned the tournament officials and withdrew.

The week certainly wasn't squandered, however, as the family had a great time on the trip, and it's not often these days I can spend a whole week with my wife and kids together. I didn't let the fact that my hip was weak get me down, but I was concerned. My surgeon had told me it was going to take time and that I was doing well and to be patient.

When I arrived in St. Louis on Monday night, July 26, for the week of the U.S. Senior Open, the most prestigious tournament in the world for guys fifty and over, it had been just ninety-seven days since I'd had major hip surgery. I had played only five competitive rounds in all that time, and more often than not been unable to walk eighteen holes. My odds on finishing the tournament would have been way less than 50–50; my odds on winning, minuscule. The one thing I had going for me was that my golf swing felt great, my putting stroke felt good, and I knew in my heart I had the game to compete. If only I could keep my tires from blowing out. . . .

I told my caddie Mike O'Connell that it was important that I play and walk a full eighteen-hole practice round on Tuesday, to really give my hip a test. I had stretched a lot during the week in Ireland and had done all the things I was supposed to do in my recovery regimen, but it was up to God and nature at that point whether I was really ready to compete.

I started on the back nine and played with Craig Stadler and Tom Purtzer, and I felt fine. They had finished their rounds, so I headed over to the first hole, just Mike and I. I really wanted to play all eighteen, as much to test the hip as to see the course. I got through about four holes and started to cramp a little, but because it was a practice round I stopped and did an abbreviated Richard Simmons routine. I pretended I was sweatin' to the oldies, but I tried to hold down the squealing. I lay on the tee and did full-torso stretches and really lengthened my hamstrings, and then got up and hit my tee shot and felt fine again. So I finished all eighteen, I was hitting the ball great, and I realized it was the most comfortable I'd felt playing a full round since the surgery. Things were going in the right direction.

On Wednesday I decided to play only nine holes, then I went to the range and practiced. I hit some balls, chipped and putted for a while, then got out of there. I had a long haul ahead and didn't want to strain myself unnecessarily before the starting gun went off.

In the first round Thursday, I was paired with Frank Connor and Alan Doyle, and it couldn't have gone any better. It was a great day, and I played a nearly flawless round of golf. I think I missed one fairway and I hit a ton of greens and putted well and shot 65. I had the lead all by myself—and this on a course that had hosted a U.S. Open in 1965, won by Gary Player, and a PGA in 1992, won by Nick Price. Bellerive was a great and stern test, playing at over 7,100 yards, and at least that day, I passed it with flying colors.

I was proud of myself for making all eighteen, and especially for being patient and not trying to overdo it. I got to the last four holes that day and was starting to cramp a little, so I played pretty conservatively. On number 17, a long par 5, I hit a good drive about 290 yards and had a chance to go for the green in two, but I laid up, though not without taking flack from some yahoos in the gallery. There's something about a major tournament that brings out— shall we say—a more eclectic group of fans. They're often more interested in the party than the golf, and it can require an extra dimension of concentration for those of us inside the ropes. Some guys were yelling "Go for it! Go for it!" But I had 250 to the green, there was water on the right front, and I had just a fair lie. I told Mike that normally I would give it a go, but I was cramping and needed to be smart about this. By laying up, I still would have a good birdie chance and I'd take bogey or double bogey out of the equation. He agreed, and when I hit a safe seven-iron to about 100 yards from the green, some hot dog in the gallery yelled, "Hey, way to go for it. That's the way to play aggressive, Jake." Obviously, now that I'm fifty I have learned to filter out the first thing that comes into my brain before it reaches my mouth. The devil on my left shoulder was telling me to say, "Hey, dickhead. Come on out here and let's see what you've got! Do you think flying a three-wood out of a poor lie 250 yards over water in a U.S. Senior Open with a cramping hip is a picnic?" But the angel won out and this is how I responded: "I'm down to my last ball and I don't want to risk it."

I got a couple of sympathy laughs and some nice applause from the gallery when I said it, but even better, the strategy worked perfectly. I hit a wedge third shot about 15 feet from the pin and made the putt for birdie, which gave me a one-shot lead at the end of the day.

After the round, I went straight to the media room to do interviews, which I always enjoy, but I knew my hip was going to tighten up quite a bit sitting there. There were the basic questions about how I had shot the score, where I made birdies, etc., but then someone asked me what my goal was for the week. Because I had a late-early tee time split, I told the writer that my only goal was to be able to show up and play at 8:05 in the morning—and I had a real concern about that. It was difficult just getting up from the chair after the interview. The leg had already started to cramp up. But I did the things I was supposed to do. I stretched in the locker room, took a hot bath, and did a workout. I didn't feel the need to hit balls, because my swing felt great. Nevertheless, when I went to bed Thursday night, I was honestly afraid I wouldn't be able to play the next day, and I found myself thinking what a shame that would be.

I woke up on Friday morning a little before six A.M. and peeked out the window. It was raining cats, dogs, emus, and Komodo dragons. It had poured down about four inches in the preceding few hours, so it was highly likely there would be a rain delay. I called the tournament headquarters, and because it was still dark outside, everything was still on "go." That was only because the officials couldn't yet see how much flooding had occurred. By seven A.M., I was ready to leave the room when I received a call that all tee times had been pushed back two hours. I took that as a good omen. It meant more rest and more time to stretch.

At ten-thirty, about the time they called off play for the whole day, I got a call on my cell phone from a strange voice. The man said, "Mr. Jacobsen, this is Tom Meeks with the USGA. We have had a change of heart about the rain delay. We're going to take a third of the field and play them in a nine-hole shotgun to get in some golf. If you are not on the first tee in ten minutes, you're disqualified."

It was a nice fakeout, but I knew all along it was Jay Haas. I'd know his voice in a rain forest. I love those kinds of prank calls between friends.

With the day washed out, I wondered whether that was going to mean thirty-six holes on Sunday, and that naturally worried me. It was a helluva challenge for me to finish eighteen, so to be out there for nine or ten hours was a big concern. However, that decision was out of my control.

Jan and Mike O'Connell and I went to a movie to relax, and who should we bump into but Bob Gilder and Tom Watson, and then in walked Alan Doyle, with whom I was paired, and Gil Morgan. Sometimes it feels like the world of professional golf is pretty insulated because we're always running into each other at dinner or the movies. You never really feel like you're totally away from home because there's always a friend or fellow competitor nearby who is part of this traveling circus of professional golf.

The choice then was to either go back to the hotel and do more stretching and exercising or go to the course to practice. The Bellerive facilities opened around three-thirty for those who wanted to practice, but I passed on that idea. Whenever you go back to the course after a rain delay, especially during a major and especially when you're leading, the media guys and gals are there. Despite the rainout, they still have stories to file, and I was sure the worst thing I could do was stand around and answer a lot of questions, which would be murder on my hip. So I returned to the hotel and worked out, and stretched and stretched and stretched. I hadn't given a thought to winning the tournament yet. My goal was to play seventy-two holes, and I literally had to take it one hour at a time and not do anything stupid.

Saturday the weather returned to normal, and I felt fairly loose going off at 8:05. It was a nice round, very comfortable, and I played well but didn't light it up like on Thursday. Nevertheless, my 1-under-par round of 70 left me tied with Stadler for the lead after thirty-six holes; more important, my hip held up fine. I had made it through two rounds in good shape, but there was trouble on the horizon. It was indeed announced by the USGA officials Saturday afternoon that we would play thirty-six holes on Sunday and finish the tournament. I had of course been hoping for a Sunday-Monday finish. My first thought was that I couldn't walk thirty-six and that I was probably going to have to withdraw. Longtime golf fans will recall that the U.S. Open on the PGA Tour always used to finish with thirty-six holes in one day, and many remember those pictures from 1964 of Ken Venturi at Congressional Country Club in Washington, D.C., suffering heat exhaustion the final day and nearly staggering up the 18th hole to win the Open. I had visions of the same thing happening if I tried to go the distance.

When I got to the first tee on Sunday, Walter Driver, the chairman of the Competitions Committee for the USGA, was there. I was paired with Stadler and Jose Maria Canizares from Spain. Walter wished me luck, and I thanked him and asked if I could talk to him for a moment. I told him that I knew we were not going to re-pair the groups because we were going thirty-six holes, and that there was a real chance I might have to pull out at some point. I told him that my hip was very iffy for going the distance. The day before, when the decision had been announced, I read that Driver told the media, "Look, if I can walk thirty-six holes in a day, then they can do it, too." And what I said to the media was, "Well, that's easy for Walter to say, but what would he shoot?"

We not only had to walk ten miles, but we had to hit quality golf shots and maintain our composure and concentration for at least nine hours. That's no small mission for old farts, but that was the reality of the situation, so I tried to be positive and told myself that although I had a bum leg, I was one of the two or three youngest guys in the field, so perhaps the long day might take an even greater toll on the older guys.

We teed off for the third round, and once again, I was really pleased with my play. I shot a solid 69, but Tom Kite had a great round of 65 and jumped ahead of me by two shots. He was minus 11 after fifty-four holes, and I was minus 9. The heat index was up there around 100 degrees with the humidity, which really helped my hip stay loose, but the sweltering combination of heat and humidity was killing me. I had gained about ten pounds during my convalescence from the surgery, and I was sweating like a coal miner.

I used the time between rounds wisely. We had less than an hour to grab a bite or practice or just rest, but instead of doing any of those things I went into the locker room and literally peeled off my shirt, pants, and underwear, and turned on a shower. I sat on the floor of the shower and started with lukewarm water and let it get colder and colder until it was very brisk. I wanted to cool myself down and make my body feel like it was about to start a new day. I was playing a mental game with myself so I wouldn't feel like I was in the middle of a marathon. I lay flat on the floor of the shower and closed my eyes and got myself in the right frame of mind for the final push. Now there are several reasons why a guy would take a cold shower, and while I admit that Bellerive is the kind of golf course that turns me on, it wasn't *that* kind of cold shower.

The locker room was empty by then. Everyone had either teed off or was outside hitting their last practice putts, so I got out of the shower and lay on the carpet and went through my stretching reg-

Chuck "the Hit Man" Hiter drills a line drive at a Fred Meyer Challenge clinic, with assistance from Jack Nicklaus and a somewhat apprehensive Arnold Palmer. *(Tom Trieck Photography)*

With Brad Faxon and Ben Crenshaw at the 1995 Ryder Cup. *(Jan Jacobsen)*

With Bill Murray and Chris Berman before the 2003 Greater Hartford Open. They had a surprise for me—and I had a surprise for them. *(Hersul/Lisa)*

Kristen leaping into my arms after my victory at the 2003 Greater Hartford Open. *(Getty Images)*

Winning the 2004 U.S. Senior Open, an amazing thrill. *(USGA Images)*

Fuzzy Zoeller and John Daly at a Fred Meyer Challenge clinic. Watch out!
(*Tom Trieck Photography*)

With my longtime Pebble Beach partner Jack Lemmon, at the 18th hole of his last AT&T.
(*Mitch Haddad*)

With Matt Griesser, aka "Sign Boy." (*Tom Trieck Photography*)

The gang at Guantanamo Bay, including Hootie & the Blowfish. (*Jay Kossoff*)

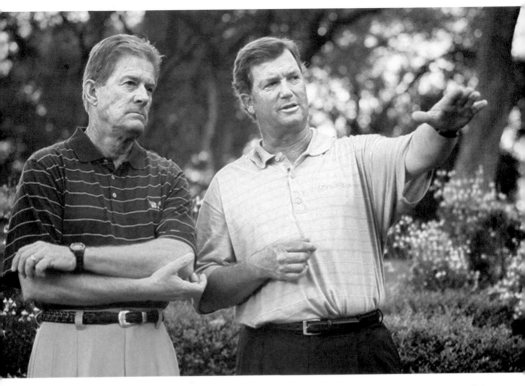

With Jim Hardy, my swing instructor and partner in golf course design. *(Rick Hunter Photography)*

With Fluff Cowan at Torrey Pines, 2002. *(Jules Alexander)*

Jake Trout and the Flounders, Mark Lye on the left, the late great Payne Stewart on the right. *(The Golf Channel)*

At the 2004 CVS Charity Classic.
What could be better than golf . . . ?
(Tom Trieck Photography)

. . . Except my family. Singing to Jan at her surprise fortieth birthday party. A Rod Stewart impersonator helps out (and I can use all the help I can get). *(Jacobsen family photo)*

The Jacobsens at Portrush, Ireland, for the 2004 Senior British Open. From left, Kristen, Mick, Amy, me, and Jan. *(Mike Cowan)*

imen. It was so relaxing, almost like I was in the eye of a hurricane. I had left a tumultuous crowd scene an hour before, had enjoyed a period of total tranquillity, and was about to ride the storm again.

I slowly put on a new set of clothes and went into the eating area and grabbed a sandwich with Bob Murphy. I sat down at the table and rather quietly said, "Bob."

He nodded and said, "Peter." We just kind of looked at each other, and if there were a cartoon bubble over our heads, it would have shown us thinking, "F———, can you believe we've gotta go do that *again*!"

I knew Murph had saved a great par on his final hole on Saturday to make the thirty-six-hole cut right on the number and there was a part of him probably wondering, Why the hell did I have to make that last putt? I could be sitting in a comfortable, temperature-controlled broadcast booth laughing at these other poor bastards, rather than going through it myself.

Bob had a towel over his shoulder, and looked like a club fighter who'd given everything he had in a battle against a ranked contender, and was now wondering if he could survive until the final bell.

I took the last bite of my sandwich and walked out of the clubhouse and into the teeming crowd. I could hear shouts of "Jake, Jake, go get 'em, buddy! How ya feelin', pal? It's your turn, Jake." It was one of those moments that struck me about the arena we live and work in. Fifteen minutes before, I'd been lying on a shower floor, buck naked, alone with my thoughts, at peace with the world, and suddenly here I was under the big microscope, tens of thousands of people watching every move, wondering if I was going to crack a funny line, looking in my eyes to see if I was going to throw up my tuna on rye because I'm in contention in a United States Golf Association championship and I've never before won a tournament that had the word "major" in front of it. And I was loving every minute of it.

And there were another 10 million people watching at home, with Johnny Miller and Dan Hicks pondering the question whether "the court jester," as Johnny called me, had enough steel in his spine to win a major tournament for the first time in his life. I knew in my heart I had the game, and the composure, to pull it off, but once again my overriding concern at that moment was whether I could complete the final round.

When I got to the tee, there was Walter Driver again, and also Fred Ridley, president of the USGA. Fred is a former U.S. Amateur champion and a contemporary of mine. We played college golf against each other in the early seventies. I told Fred the same thing I had told Walter five hours prior, that I hoped I could get in all eighteen, but that I might not make it. I wasn't being melodramatic; I just wanted to give fair warning so he wouldn't be alarmed if I pulled up like an old mare in an Irish sweeps race. I would have rated my chances of finishing at about 50–50 at that moment. Remember, the pattern had been that after about fourteen holes I would cramp up. The first round had taken over four and a half hours, and we were looking at about the same span for this one.

My first words to my caddie, Mike, were, "Let's see how far we can go. Let's gut this thing out."

Mike didn't mince words. He had fire in his eyes and said, "Yeah, let's win this goddamn thing!"

His words pumped me up, but I also knew I had to stay relaxed and patient, and take the round not only one hole at a time, but one step at a time.

I absolutely killed my drive off the first tee, hit an eight-iron in there about 12 feet and made the putt for birdie. That gave me a boost of confidence and got the adrenaline flowing. The second hole was a carbon copy of the first: three-wood, wedge to 12 feet, birdie. Two holes, two birdies, and in the group ahead, Tom Kite had made a bogey so I was back in the lead. On number 3, I was pumped up and hit a nine-iron into the left corner of the green, and the ball jumped into a back bunker. I had a very tough bunker shot and I was thinking, Don't give back one of those hard-fought birdies and sacrifice any momentum. Natural adrenaline was the best drug possible for my hip at that point, and I didn't want to do anything that would cause me to lose it. Sure enough, I hit a good bunker shot to about 8 feet and made another nice putt for par. Three holes, three one-putts. Me *likee*!

I made pars on the 4th and 5th holes, but when I got to the 6th tee, a tough par 3 over water, there was a big backup. Hale Irwin, the most dominant player in the history of the Champions Tour, had hit his shot in the water and was making a big number, and there were two or three groups on the tee ahead of us. It was going to be about a twenty-five-minute holdup, so I headed over to a spot under a tree. I wanted to turn a potential curse into a blessing and use the time well by doing some stretching. Fuzzy Zoeller was on the tee. I consider Fuzzy one of the truly great guys in golf, and as I walked by, in his typically irreverent way, he said, "Hey, Jake. Stop your walking. You come back up here." So I walked back up the hill with Fuzzy, under the shade of a tree. "You feel that breeze?" he said. "I ordered that especially for us."

Fuzzy's probably the calmest guy on Tour, and just talking to him is relaxing, so I enjoyed our little visit. I did some light stretching, and then he walked down to the tee to hit. I was standing in the crosswalk going down to the 6th tee, sweating so bad I looked like I was lactating. I had these big sweat stains around my chest, and a fan behind the ropes, with a beer in each hand, came out with this truly original line. He yelled, "Hey, Peter, is it hot enough for ya?"

So I walked over to him and said, "Now, what kind of a question is that? I'm standing here looking like I just dove in a pool. It's a hundred degrees out here and you ask me a stupid question like that." I said it with a grin, really just making conversation to pass the time. And then I said, "The question you need to ask a guy like me when you're standing here with two beers in your hand is 'Hey, Peter, want a pull on my Budweiser?'" The people around us were laughing now, and the guy got all excited and said, "Okay, you want a pull?"

And I said, "Damn right I do." And I grabbed one of his beers and took a couple good chugs from it and handed it back to him. "Now that's what you ask a fat sweaty guy on the sixth tee of the U.S. Senior Open," I said. And the guy was really fired up then and said, "Oh man, I hope that helps you win! I hope that helps you win!"

That was the kind of friendly exchange with the gallery that is so important to the growth of the PGA Tour and the Champions Tour. I always try to do that sort of thing when the opportunity arises because that kind of interaction is just part of my personality, but I know that for a lot of guys it's an awkward and difficult thing to do. We all need to make some sort of effort, though, because it's easy for fans to get turned off to dial-tone personalities.

When our turn arrived to pull the trigger on number 6, I hit a conservative shot to the middle of the green. Guys were making bogeys and double-bogeys galore on this hole, so even though I three-putted for bogey, I considered the hole a push. The wait on the tee had been helpful and I wasn't feeling any pain in my hip. A nice birdie on the 7th hole, and solid pars on 8 and 9, left me two behind Kite at 11 under par as we made the turn.

There were nine holes to go and I was in the hunt, but I still had lingering doubts about whether I could go for another two hours plus. I still wasn't thinking about winning the tournament at that point; rather, I was keeping my thoughts in the present and having fun. I had told Johnny Miller in the broadcast booth the day before, when he'd been giving me a friendly lecture about putting on my game face and treating the Senior Open like serious business, that it was still fun for me, and that I would never treat it too seriously. And I was determined to stay that way. I knew I was swinging well and that my coach Jim Hardy was watching me on the tube back home in Houston, and I wanted to impress him with every swing.

The 10th was another critical hole for me. It's a par 5 for the members that the USGA turns into a par 4 for competitions, and I birdied it with a 40-foot downhill seagoer. When a putt like that drops, you start to think it might be your week. It looked even more that way when I hit a wedge to 5 feet on number 11 to go 13 under. Kite was also stringing birdies, however, so the lead was going back and forth. On the 12th, as we were walking off the tee, I told Mike, "My hip doesn't hurt a bit," and I really didn't think about it again the rest of the round. I was now fully engaged in battle, the humidity was helping, and I could feel the adrenaline pumping. This was the type of situation a player lives for—going head-to-head on a great course with Hall of Famers like Kite and Irwin in a major championship. You learn more about yourself at times like that than at any other, and I was really excited and more than grateful to be in that position.

My drive on 12 landed in the left rough by a yard, and we're talking spinach here, and not the kind that swelled Popeye's biceps. I played the only logical shot, a layup short of the green, and was left with a tough blast/pitch over a bunker and made bogey. Kite still had the lead. I made a routine par on number 13, and then a key birdie on 14, where I hit a nine-iron second shot to 15 feet and nailed the putt. I kept hearing roars and watching Kite make putts ahead of us, but I didn't know that Miller and the other commentators were saying that his putting stroke didn't look good, that he was somehow getting putts in the hole with a stroke that looked like it was feeling the heat.

But I couldn't worry about Tom. I had plenty of work left myself, and my confidence was still very high. On the 15th, one stroke back, I was faced with the hardest driving hole on the course. It's a dogleg to the right and the fairway slopes dramatically left, so the design demands that you hit a slice. The hole sets up perfectly for Stadler, because he hits this nice fade over the bunkers. It wasn't perfect for me, and when I hit a straight ball over the bunker with no fade, it rolled down into the rough. Again, the lie was like hitting out of a Cobb salad, minus the olives and blue cheese. I managed to hit a low, running seven-iron that made it into the right bunker, a long way from the hole. I blasted out and two-putted for bogey. I was now back to 12 under, and Kite, up ahead, was at 13 because he had also bogeyed the 15th hole. Hale Irwin was at 11 under at that point and certainly a factor in the tournament. And Jay Haas was lingering near the lead as well.

These were all guys who knew how to win. Irwin had three U.S. Opens and two Senior Opens under his belt, and he had said at the beginning of the week that he wanted that third Senior Open badly. Kite had won the infamous U.S. Open at Pebble Beach in 1992, the one where Gil Morgan had become the first man ever to reach double figures under par in an Open, but then by the end of the week, because of strong winds and baked-out greens, not one player in the field had been able to finish seventy-two holes at even par. Jay Haas was playing like he was twenty-five again, regularly racking up top tens on the PGA Tour, and he would be named to the U.S. Ryder Cup team two weeks later.

And me? Well, as Dan Hicks had pointed out, I had won the U.S. Open only in *Tin Cup*. While I had won seven PGA Tour events, including Hartford only the year before, I had never won a tournament that was considered a major championship and I had never won a USGA title. I knew there were doubters who didn't think I could win this one, either.

The night before, Jay Randolph, the veteran broadcaster and a St. Louis icon, a guy sometimes referred to as the Round Mound of Sound, had said on a local network that I wouldn't win the Senior Open because my hip was in question and because I hadn't been in a leading position in a major before, the way Kite and Irwin had. Jay wasn't being malicious about it; he was just making his pick and you couldn't fault his logic. But that gave me the motivation to prove him wrong, and I also wanted to prove to my pal Johnny Miller that I could win a big one and have a blast doing it. There was no question I was having a great time out there down the stretch, but there was a big question as to whether I could close the deal.

The 16th hole at Bellerive is a very difficult par 3, 235 yards, with a big green, and the pin was cut on the right front in a place that's hard to reach from the tee. It's not a pin you shoot at unless it's your final hole and you have to make birdie. I hit a pretty good three-iron to the middle of the green, about 60 feet away, and I had an extremely tough putt with about 15 feet of break. I hit the putt pretty good but a touch soft, and it stopped 12 feet above the hole. It was not the kind of putt you want to leave yourself, because if I gave the second putt a good run it would scoot 5 feet past and I could end up with a four-putt. This was a spot where I had to fight off demons. I'd just bogeyed 15, and now was in a position to make bogey or worse on 16, which would very likely cost me the tournament. The negative thoughts were trying to creep in, but I just focused on the task at hand and hit maybe the best clutch putt of my life. It melted into the dead center like butter on a hot roll. Kite had bogeyed 16, so when I walked off the green I was tied for the lead once again and felt more strongly than ever that I could win the tournament.

I ripped a drive on 17, the par 5, but the hole was playing long so I laid up to a good wedge distance, then threw one in there about 12 feet short of the hole. I hit a good birdie putt, but it just died off to the right. As I walked to the 18th tee, I saw that I was still tied with Kite, at 12 under, and that Irwin was in the clubhouse at minus 11. Jay Haas was at 10 under. Kite and Haas had already hit their second shots on the final hole before I approached the tee, so I didn't know what had happened with their drives. I was aware at that moment that a playoff was likely, and it wasn't an appealing thought because the Senior Open requires a four-hole playoff. I wasn't thinking negatively about a playoff, but it certainly wasn't my first choice, having already gone thirty-six holes on a shaky hip.

The 18th is one of the best and most strategic holes at Bellerive. It's a dogleg left par 4, and there is a bunker on the corner of the dogleg that requires about 265 yards to carry. A lot of players throughout the week had been suckered into driving the ball over the bunker and paid the price. Stadler had done it in our morning round, and Craig had carried it far enough to where he had a wedge to the green. To me, it was just too much of a gamble with not enough reward. My goal was simple: to get the ball on the fairway with a clear shot to the green. I didn't know what was happening up ahead, but I knew I didn't want to beat myself outright or lose the opportunity for a playoff. I hit a three-wood straight down the middle and killed it. I couldn't have drawn it up better on a dream chart. As we were walking to the ball, I said to Mike, "Okay, let's make birdie here. We'll go for the flag, we've been doing that all day."

And Mike reinforced my positive thoughts by saying, "I like that. You're swinging great, you're putting well."

We got to the ball and had exactly 170 yards to the pin, right on the nose. I heard someone in the gallery say, "Jake, you're going to win it. Kite's making a bundle."

But you can never believe reports like that. For all I knew, it was the same guy who had said on the 17th hole of the first round "Nice layup" when I chose not to go for the green in two. So Mike walked over to a friend of his in the gallery and asked, "Is Kite making a big number?"

And his friend nodded and said that Kite was facing a 15-foot putt for bogey. Just then I saw Tom hit the putt and you could hear people go "Awwww!" While I didn't know for sure what he'd made, I could tell by the crowd reaction and the way Kite hung his head walking to the hole that it probably wasn't just a bogey. The murmuring from the crowd had pity etched all over it. Then Mike walked back over and confirmed that Tom had made 6. He reported that Irwin was in the clubhouse at 11 under. I simply said, "Okay," but it hit me immediately that if I made par I'd win the U.S. Senior Open. That was a great realization, but again I couldn't let it affect me. I had to protect against an adrenaline rush or any false sense of comfort that the tournament was in the bag.

In 1988, I'd stood in the 18th fairway at Butler National on the 72nd hole of the Western Open with a one-shot lead and a six-iron in my hand. I let some funny thoughts creep in, and ended up finding a water hazard behind the green. I made a double bogey and gave the title to a totally unknown player named Jim Benepe, who was in the tournament on a sponsor's exemption. It was one of my most painful memories as a professional. Experience is a great teacher, and so I just kept my thoughts focused on the present shot and was resolved to stay with the plan that had gotten me this far.

I took out a seven-iron and felt that it was the perfect club for 170 yards and for feeling slightly pumped up. Mike said, "What's your line?" And I said, "Right at it." I was so confident in my golf swing I really didn't give a thought to playing the shot to the fat part of the green, where I could be left with a 40-footer with a huge break. So many times when you try to make a par, you end up with a bogey. My thinking was, I'm going to try to stiff this shot and if I don't make birdie I'll make par. That's extremely positive thinking, but that's where my head was right then. I'd hit crisp, true iron shots all week. I needed just one more.

I hit that seven-iron so perfect it felt like a practice swing. In golf we talk about "dotting the i," when the ball hangs straight over the flagstick. It looked in the air like it was going in the hole. It landed just past the flag and started trickling to the left. The gallery gave a huge cheer, but I wasn't ready to do the Macarena or reenact Chi Chi's saber dance just yet. Besides, either one of those moves would have dislocated my hip. I knew that I still had an extremely tough two-putt waiting for me, and if I wasn't able to execute it I would be going into a four-hole playoff with homeboy Hale Irwin, a local god in St. Louis with five U.S. Open and Senior Open crowns under his belt. I discovered later that the boys in the booth were saying that I had left my ball in a very vulnerable position. And they were right. I had a 25-foot downhiller with a huge break in it. The slightest miscue and I could knock the putt 8 feet by.

Some guy in the grandstand yelled out, "Hey, Jake, how does it feel to win your first major?" Now I've heard stories about how Jack Nicklaus in his prime was so locked into the moment that he wouldn't hear a pistol shot when he was in competition. But I can hear a mosquito fart. I heard the guy's comment loud and clear, but I had absolutely no interest in responding to it. I still had a lot of work to do.

When I took my first look at the putt, I said, "Mike, I think this is breaking about five feet." And he said, "No, it's much more." He pointed way left of Stadler's coin, which was about 4 feet left of the hole. And he was right on the money. It was about a 10-foot break and the amount it moved would be totally dependent on the speed. After a lifetime in this sport, you learn that there are certain lessons you can go back to when the pressure ratchets up, and my friend Chuck Hogan, a great teacher of the mental side of golf, had always drilled into me that there's a "big picture" and a "little picture." The big picture would have been for me to stand there preparing my victory speech, and mentally listing whom I was going to thank.

If my mind had wandered like that, however, I might have four-putted. I needed to stay in what Chuck called "the little picture," which was the immediate challenge of getting this dangerous putt down in two. I had to carefully pick my line, feel the speed, and trust my stroke to do the rest. There would be plenty of time for speech writing while I was signing my scorecard and cooling down.

I went through my routine, staying totally in the little picture, and hit a great putt. It fell down the break line perfectly, and I thought for a second I'd holed it. But it slid by the right edge and kept inching past, and I was thinking to myself, Whoa, whoa . . . It finally came to a stop 2 feet away. I marked it and had to wait for Craig and Jose Maria to finish out, and I never once took my mind off that 2-footer. Every golfer alive has missed two-footers, so I certainly wasn't taking it for granted. After what seemed a long time, I went up, put my ball back, picked up my coin, and said to Mike, "There's nothing to this. It's straight in." And he said, "Absolutely."

Mike backed away and the funny thing was that, as I was standing over the putt and knocking it in, I didn't know until I reviewed the tape later that Mike was standing behind me, struggling to get the 18th hole flag off the flagstick. It's a tradition in golf for caddies, especially in majors, to capture that flag as their great me-

mento of the victory. It's sort of like one of Sitting Bull's braves tucking a scalp under his belt at Little Big Horn.

I teased Mike later and said, "You son of a bitch, the whole time I'm hitting the putt to win the tournament, you were wrestling with that flag." And he shrugged and said, "Ah, I knew you were going to make it."

The crowd gave me a great ovation when I holed out, and I was just flying. The natural adrenaline was kicking in, and I didn't have a hint of pain. Roger Maltbie, NBC's outstanding fairway rover, has been a great pal of mine for years, and he came over and said, "Jake, you got it done, man. You walked thirty-six and you had fun doing it." It was a jovial jab at Johnny Miller, and so I followed Roger's comment with "See, Johnny, I told you this was fun and games for me. I had a good time and I ended up winning." It was all in good spirits, but in fact I had used Johnny's comments and those of Jay Randolph as motivational tools. The next day, when I reviewed the tape, I heard Johnny say, "I have to believe that ninety-nine percent of the golfing public wants to see Peter Jacobsen win this thing." Johnny's been a great friend to me for many years, and his generous comment meant a lot.

I also told Roger on the 18th green that I'd had a wonderful career, and I was honored to share it with a lot of people. I was inspired by Arnold Palmer's interview at the Masters when he'd completed his fiftieth appearance at Augusta, and said how he wouldn't take any credit for what he'd accomplished, but that he owed everything to the fans. All of us on the Tour should never forget how our careers touch other people, and how when we win, it brings pleasure and excitement to all those who are in our lives on a daily basis: our families, teachers, business associates, amateur pro-am partners, neighbors, and on and on. Within two days of the victory, I took about 150 voice mails off my cell phone and had nearly twice as many e-mails from friends congratulating me. It takes a while to get back to all those people, but it's something I try to do. Whether it's a celebration of a victory or an accomplishment, or condolences offered during a hard time, when people call or send a note, I believe they are entitled to hear back.

After I'd spoken with Maltbie, Jan came over and hugged me and gave me a kiss—you know it's love when your wife kisses you when you're that sweaty and stinky—and we shared one of those looks that says it all. We both knew what the last one hundred days had been like. Jan had been unbelievably great in the days after the operation, when I'd needed her help for even the most basic of things. Three months before, it had looked like my rookie season on the Champions Tour might be a complete washout, and here I was with her, about to be presented the top prize in senior golf. Wow!

I was asked where I would rank the U.S. Senior Open on my playing résumé, and that's not easy to answer. I've been playing in USGA events for thirty-five years. I'd played in two national junior championships, four national amateurs, and probably fifteen to twenty U.S. Opens before I turned fifty, and had never won one. So to have a national title on my résumé was incredible.

I would say my biggest thrill in golf was winning my first PGA Tour event, in 1980 at the Buick Open. That one broke the ice for me and totally validated my choice to play the Tour.

My most inspirational victory came in 1984 when I went to the Colonial Invitational in Fort Worth with the express purpose of winning the tournament for my father, Erling Jacobsen, who I thought was not going to make it through the week because of his cancer. I beat my pal Payne Stewart in a playoff and dedicated the win to my dad. That's funny in a way, because one of the great perks of winning the '04 Senior Open is that it gave me an exemption for the 2005 U.S. Open at Pinehurst, the site of Payne's last victory in 1999, when he made that amazing 15-footer for par on the final green and punched his fist into the air. They've erected a statue commemorating that moment at Pinehurst. It's going to be very emotional to see that. I know I'll cry, but that's all right. I loved the guy.

Probably the most gratifying win came in 2003 at Hartford, when at age forty-nine I was somehow able to raise my game and beat a great field on the regular PGA Tour in front of fans I'd come to love so much since I first won at Hartford nineteen years earlier.

I'd definitely rank the U.S. Senior Open as the most unexpected win of my career, a huge thrill, and probably the most fun. When I look at the trophy today and see the names of so many of my heroes ... Arnold and Jack and Gary and Lee and Sam and Hale ... wow ... it really hits me what I've done.

I pity my embalmer some forty years from now, when I keel over in a bunker at Armadillo Pitch-and-Putt. Even then, he's going to have a helluva time getting the grin off my face.

9

The Pros and the Ams

I GOT TO KNOW Vijay Singh fairly well in the mid-nineties. I would be hitting balls on the range, and because he was always somewhere on the practice facility working on his game, many times I would be hitting right next to him. One day he said to me, "Man, you're hitting it so good you're like that machine, Iron Byron."

And I said, "Look at you. Every divot is exactly the same. Every ball flight is exactly the same. If anyone is Iron Byron, it's you."

And so for about two years every time I'd see him it was "Hey, Iron." And he'd go, "What's up, Byron?" Or vice versa. And then the joke sorta wears off and you end up using your real names.

It's been fascinating to watch Vijay apply his incredible work ethic—and for the last five or six years a grueling fitness regimen that has turned him into one of the two or three best conditioned players in golf—to become the number-one player in the world.

Whenever three or four players are sitting around having dinner, or just a casual cocktail, and Vijay's name comes up, the main topic of conversation is the respect they have for him. They don't talk about his impact on TV ratings or how he could be better with the media, they talk about his golf game and how misunderstood he is. They discuss his swing or his short game or his competitiveness or how he goes from one style putter to another overnight and makes darn near everything he looks at no matter what putter he's using.

The players appreciate what Vijay has done to get to where he is today, and despite what you might read about any elusiveness or bitterness toward the press, among the players he's one of the most popular guys on Tour. I think he's been treated rather harshly because he rose to the number-one position after Tiger had dominated the top of the golfing world for about seven years, and there's never been a more charismatic or dramatic golfer to watch coming down the stretch than Woods. In the fifty years that golf has been televised, there are only two players whose presence on a leader board has dramatically spiked ratings—Arnold Palmer and Tiger. So when they write that Vijay is not good for ratings, it's because he's being compared to a guy who should have Nielsen for a middle name. He may not be as telegenic as Tiger, but then who is? Any golfer who believes that old adage that "you find your game in the dirt" has to appreciate the discipline and desire that are behind Vijay Singh's rise to the top.

In addition, although he may not be the most jovial guy in the world in a press conference, the other players will tell you that Vijay has a delightful personality, and that he's very generous with sharing information about things he's learned. I don't know how many times I've seen him walk over to a new player or someone he might not even know (he peeks at the guy's bag to learn his name) and say, "Hey, bro, what's up? How you hitting it?"

And if the guy doesn't know Vijay, he'll immediately perk up and think, Wow, Vijay Singh is talking to me. The next thing you know, Vijay is giving the guy a lesson. He might spend a half hour with him, sharing a nifty little shot he's learned or showing the guy another way to play a pitch shot or a buried lie in a bunker. Yet the press, and through them the public, sometimes has this perception of Vijay as kind of a surly guy.

I'll never forget the ADT Skills Challenge in Naples, Florida, in 2002—I think that was where people got a glimpse of both the talent and the personality of Vijay. In the Skills Challenge, ten players hit a bunch of different shots—middle irons, short irons, long drives, bunker shots, trouble shots, etc.—and amass dollars based on how they finish in each competition. Vijay was leading coming to the last shot, which was a short iron over water. We hit in inverse order, so when it was his turn to hit, he only needed to get one of the three balls within 12 feet to win the overall title. He managed it on his first shot, and the TV announcers started to put the ribbon on the broadcast and declare him the winner.

But Vijay wanted to win this final competition, which would add to his money total, so he requested that he be allowed to hit his final two balls. He turned to Mike Weir, a left-hander, and said, "Can I use your eight-iron?" He then turned around and put this absolutely pure southpaw swing on it and flushed it in there 2 feet from the hole. All of us in the competition fell to our knees and gave him the "We're Not Worthy" bow from *Wayne's World.* Vijay got the biggest smile on his face that you've ever seen. Now that's the playful and ultra-talented Vijay Singh the guys on Tour have come to know.

It's clear to me that Vijay's public image could easily be fixed. The powers that be in golf could call in Vijay and say, "Veej, you are the Man right now in golf. You won nine times in 2004, you've won three majors and are going to win more, and yet you're very misunderstood by the general golfing public. So we are going to put you at the very center of our marketing campaign for the PGA Tour for the next twelve or eighteen months, and we're going to help inform the public about your great story and your unmatched work ethic. But you have to work with us. You have to be more open with the media, let them see the playful side of your personality, and become an example of how any kid with enough desire, no matter the circumstances of his upbringing, can reach the top of this sport."

I'll bet you Vijay would get on board with that program, because I'm certain he would like to improve the perception people have of him. Think about it. Here is a man of color, from Fiji—not exactly a golfing Mecca—who played all over the world for several years to hone his skills, and reached the top of his sport not at age twenty-five or thirty, but at forty! Now tell me that isn't an inspirational story, and one that gives people hope. The only other athlete I can think of who got better after forty is Barry Bonds, and it's just possible he may have taken some liquid shortcuts along the way.

An example of marketing gone right was when Phil Mickelson did the talk-show circuit after winning the Masters in 2004. Recognizing that he was one of the most popular champions ever, and that his dramatic victory in what's arguably the most attractive major was long overdue, his advisers booked him on *The Tonight Show with Jay Leno,* and on *David Letterman, Conan O'Brien, Regis and Kelly,* and other shows. Phil showed himself to be a fun and thoughtful guy with a great family who'd finally gotten the gorilla off his back. He went along with the jokes and ribbing about his leap on the 18th green after holing the winning putt—Phil jumped "low" in the air, arms up, then scooped the ball up, kissed it, and threw it into the crowd—a classic example of "white man's disease," some said, and he showed the general public that, like most of the top players in golf, he was a man with his priorities clearly in place. Phil's talk-show tour undoubtedly expanded his fan base among the nongolfing crowd and was very positive for our sport.

Bottom line: the same thing needs to be done for Vijay, and I'm sure his image will improve dramatically and get more in sync with who he really is.

While I'm thinking about Mickelson, one of the reasons people like Phil so much is that they can see the pleasant, boyish smile he always has on his face, which expresses how much he loves playing, yet they can also sense the fire in his belly. Just think about his demeanor as he walked up to the final green of the Masters in 2004 when he nipped Ernie Els with that dramatic final birdie. Here was a guy who'd gone something like zero for forty-six in the majors, was clearly labeled as the best player never to win a major, and had seen two players, Payne Stewart and David Toms, make great putts on the final green right in his face to snatch majors away from him. And yet if you studied Phil's face and body language, he acted like a guy who was playing in the third flight of his member-guest invitational. It was just terrific to see a guy enjoying the moment the way he was, when other players might have looked like they were heading to the doctor for a prostate exam.

Phil loves pressure, and he loves it when the stakes are meaningful. Even in practice rounds, Phil likes to have a little mustard on the line.

A few years ago at the Bob Hope Chrysler Classic, I bumped into Phil on Monday and we arranged to play a practice round the next day, just a quick nine holes at PGA West's Palmer Course. We went out there late on Tuesday afternoon, after most of the amateurs had dug their divots and gone in for a cocktail, and on the first tee Phil said, "Let's play a hundred dollars a hole."

Now I knew that he had been working hard in the off-season and had his A-game going, but I was coming out of a cold winter in Portland and was just trying to work out the kinks. I was thinking I didn't want to play for anything, but he challenged me. He said, "C'mon, the most you can lose is nine hundred bucks."

So I said, "All right, son of a bitch, you're on!"

He proceeded to take his opening drive over the corner bunker, about a 290-yard carry, and leave it 80 yards from the green. He started the first four holes birdie, eagle, birdie, birdie. Fortunately I went par, birdie, par, birdie, so I was only three down. Two under par and three down. By the time we got to the 9th hole, I'd birdied the three previous holes and had pulled even in the match. On the scorecard he was 5 under par through eight holes and so was I, and he was pissed off that he didn't have me buried. I could feel the adrenaline pumping. I could clearly see why Phil liked to have something on the line in practice rounds. It really has a way of preparing you for the competition of the tournament.

In the old days, Jackie Burke told me they used to play for significant money in practice rounds because the purses were so small that a player could make—or lose—more money on Tuesday or Wednesday than was at stake during the tournament. Nowadays you make $10,000 just by making the cut in a PGA Tour event, and you make around a million if you win the tournament, so five hundred dollars doesn't exactly stoke your fire. This match with Phil was more about pride than money, however. I'd made a couple other nice putts, and by the time we got to the 9th tee, the match was even. Phil said, "All right. We're dead square. Last hole is for five hundred bucks."

I said, "Jeez, Phil, if you're hard up for gas money I can always float you a loan." But I was feeling good and it was a lively match, so I said, "Sure, why not?"

Mickelson piped his drive about 300 yards down the middle, and I hit mine in the right rough. The hole is a difficult par 4, about 450 yards, with water all down the left side, and it's very narrow. I had to take a six-iron and hit a low running shot out to the right and just try to get up near the green. I hit it just the way I wanted and it ran up by the edge of the green and slightly over, and I was left with a tough 80-foot pitch shot back to the hole. Meanwhile,

Phil had only a wedge left, and he hit it in there to 8 feet. I was thinking, *Sayonara,* half a yard. When I hit a nice chip down there a foot from the hole, he conceded the putt, convinced, I'm sure, that he was going to drill his birdie putt. He was really bearing down on it, and made his patented aggressive stroke. The putt just missed, and rolled about three and a half feet past. He stood there for a long moment making practice strokes, wondering how he could have missed, and I didn't utter a peep. I said to my caddie Mike O'Connell, "Watch this . . . watch this."

Phil was waiting for me to say it was good, and he was kinda stalling standing there. Then finally he said, "My goodness, it's awfully quiet out here."

And because he'd put my feet to the fire, I couldn't resist jabbing back. "Well, Phil, you know all these reporters have been writing how you've missed a few shorties under pressure. I want to see if it's true."

He gave me a smile and said, "You son of a bitch . . ."

And I said, "Pick it up."

The story tells you something about Phil, what a competitor he is, and it tells you how motivated a Tour player can get when he's challenged. I remember every shot we hit in that nine-hole "friendly" match, and I'd be hard-pressed to recall every shot for nine holes in any other Tour event.

While I'm thinking of it, it would be interesting to hook up all the players on the Tour to a polygraph machine and ask them this multiple-choice question: Would you rather stand on the 18th tee with a ten-shot lead, or a one-shot lead, or be tied for the lead? Although the answer may seem obvious, the true-grit competitor would prefer to be tied for the lead, just so he could test his mettle in a pressure situation. The answer would reveal the nature of the guy's competitive drive. I guarantee you Phil is the kind of player who would like to be tied with one to play, and so is Tiger, and so is Vijay. If you asked Larry Bird, I believe he would say he prefers to be one point behind with 12 seconds to go with the ball in his hands in an NBA playoff game, because he's spent thousands of hours preparing for that moment when he'd make the winning shot, and he believes in his heart and soul that he'd make it. That challenge is much more satisfying to him than sitting on the ball with a 10-point lead.

If I were to address that question myself, my answer would vary depending on the circumstances in my career. When I was going for my first win in 1980, I know that no lead would have been big enough because I just wanted to nail down that first win and become fully exempt and reap all the benefits that a victory on the Tour affords a player. But I loved coming to the last hole of the U.S. Senior Open knowing the situation would test everything I had. That was exhilarating.

THERE'S NEVER ANY BETTING between players on tournament days in PGA or Champions Tour events, but a few years ago in the Bob Hope, I had a super-jock pairing of former NFL All-Pro wide receiver Roy Green, Michael Jordan, and Charles Barkley, and there was so much serious action going back and forth we needed a CPA to keep track of it all. I didn't mind, because tournaments like the Hope are as much about fan entertainment as anything else, and the fans were getting a huge kick out of Jordan and Barkley sticking the hypodermic needle in each other.

Jordan was playing pretty well and Barkley was playing horribly, but what would you expect from a guy whose golf swing resembles a check-swing in baseball. Just like those commercials that Tiger does with Sir Charles, after you've watched him make that double-hitch flinching spasm a couple times, you find yourself looking away for fear it's a virus that's contagious. I can appreciate what a great athlete Barkley is because he has the club in such an awkward position on the backswing that it takes incredible coordination just to get the club face back to the same zip code as the ball.

Anyway, Charles would throw down on Michael and say, "I'll bet you a thousand dollars you can't hit this fairway," and Michael would say, "I'll bet you five grand you can't clear the water with your second shot." It went back and forth all day. I asked Michael on one hole whether they were serious about the bets, and he said, "Yeah, I've got him down thirteen grand right now."

So we were on the 12th hole, and Charles hit probably his best shot of the day. It was a five-iron that made it to the fringe of a par-3 hole, about 30 feet from the cup. With his fat handicap, Charles got a stroke even on the short holes, so if he two-putted it would give our team a net birdie. The TV cameras were rolling, and about 3 million people were watching, and Michael jumped in and said, "I'll bet you ten grand you can't make par."

Now Jordan really had the nuts on that bet. Vegas would have made Charles about a 4-to-1 underdog to two-putt from the fringe, but of course Barkley couldn't look like he had cold feet so he accepted the wager. Sir Charles managed to leave his first putt about 3 feet away, which was respectable, but then Jordan started harassing him mercilessly about how he'd never convert the short one. Sure enough, Charles knocked it in, which was immediately followed by fist pumping and high-fiving and Ricky Martin dance moves that would empty a disco.

A couple holes later, on the par-3 17th, there was a guitar on the tee, because Vince Gill and Glenn Frey were playing and the idea was that they could hum a few bars while they were waiting. When our group arrived, I couldn't resist grabbing it and strumming right during Barkley's shot as he was addressing his ball. Now this, too, was broadcast live on national television, so Charles pretended it didn't bother him and went ahead and, despite all the giggling and distraction, put his vertical seizure move on it. He hit this big old shank up onto the mountains; it bounced dead left off the rocks and rolled across the green and into the water on the left side. The announcer asked what song I was playing and I said, "The Barkley Blues," because it had been a long afternoon for the Round Mound of Rebound. But then that's what tournaments like the Hope are all about—a little golf accompanied by a lot of giggles.

THERE ARE DOZENS of stories about celebrity antics from the AT&T National Pro-Am. In 2003 I was playing with my partner Huey Lewis at Spyglass Hill, on the first hole. He blocked his drive right, over by the cart path in that nasty Spyglass grass that's hard to hit out of. His buddy Deacon Lewis (no relation) was on the bag for him and there was a good crowd. Huey looked down and said, "Damn, Deacon, that's a nasty lie. Whaddaya think, five-wood or three-iron?" In his syrupy Southern drawl, Deacon said, "Ah like the lumber."

Huey said, "I dunno, Deacon. I don't hit that club very good."

Deacon, after a pregnant pause, said, "Well, you don't hit the three-iron worth a shit either."

So Huey hit sort of a fat five-wood down there, flipped the club back to his caddie, and said, "Yeah, you were right, Deacon."

I quit laughing on about the 4th green.

Most golf fans remember the year Bill Murray grabbed a woman in her seventies out of the gallery beside the 18th hole, did a quick do-si-do with her, and then watched in horror as the lady slipped from his grip and fell backward into the bunker. My first thought when I watched the tape was that he had seriously injured her, or at least ruined her day. Turns out she wasn't hurt at all, and to this day that lady faithfully follows Murray every time he plays Pebble Beach. She had a lot to cheer for in 2005 as Bill and his partner Scott Simpson finished fourth overall in the pro-am. Murray just played his butt off. I still think he has an amazing golf swing. His positions on the backswing, at impact, and on his followthrough are textbook perfect. Few people realize that Bill grew up in a big golfing family in Chicago, and that much of the film *Caddyshack,* cowritten with his brother Brian Doyle Murray, is about the Murray boys' experiences hanging out at public courses. I have a feeling that no matter how many wonderful acting performances Bill gives the rest of his life, his defining role will always be Carl Spackler, the greenskeeper who wants to make the lady members at Bushwood Country Club "bark like a dog."

Samuel L. Jackson and George Lopez are two other actors who totally understand what pro-ams are all about. As good as Jack Lemmon was with people in the gallery, I don't think I have ever played golf with a celebrity who gives as much to the crowd as Samuel does. He is an absolute gem. I've played with him in Portland and in Palm Springs, and there's inevitably a holdup in those celebrity pro-ams. Samuel will always go under the ropes and into the crowd to visit with people and sign autographs. Usually the movie stars and pros use that yellow nylon gallery rope as a kind of force field like the one on the Starship *Enterprise,* to keep the people away from them. But not Samuel. He gets out there among 'em. I asked him one time why he was doing that, and he said, "Because, Peter, these are the people who allow me to be playing here. They go see my movies, they buy the DVDs, they make me who I am. And I greatly appreciate their support of me and my work."

How impressive is that?

George Lopez constantly interacts with the fans, as well, showing elation at a good shot or mock despair if a shot doesn't go well. After holing a putt in the AT&T this last year, he did some super cool dance moves, sort of a Mexican Robot maneuver, then hit the ground in the splits. Every man over thirty in America felt his voice go up an octave. And there are so many other guys who love golf and really share it with the fans: Kevin Costner, Kurt Russell, Joe Pesci, Ray Romano, Will Smith, Kevin James—I could go on. I miss the days when we had so many top-name celebrities not only playing in these events, but even putting their names on tournaments. When I started out in the late seventies, there were about a dozen top-drawer celebs hosting tournaments. Just off the top of my head, there were Dean Martin and later Joe Garagiola in Tucson, Glen Campbell in L.A., Jackie Gleason in Florida, Bing Crosby at Pebble, Bob Hope in Palm Springs, Danny Thomas in Memphis, Andy Williams in San Diego, Ed McMahon in Quad Cities, and Sammy Davis, Jr., in Hartford.

I'll never forget when I won at Hartford the first time, in 1984, and Sammy Davis presented me with the check. I'd signed my scorecard and was walking down to the green when I saw Sammy for the first time that week. I couldn't believe how tiny he was. He looked like one of the friggin' lollipop kids from *The Wizard of Oz*. He had the tight pants and the Mister T starter kit around his neck, pure showbiz all the way. He took the microphone and said, "Hey, man. I can't wait to hand over the loot to this cat, man. Peter Jacobsen wins my tournament, man. And I hear he thinks he's an entertainer, so maybe I won't give him the microphone, man." And then he started talking to me, but he had that glass eyeball spinning in every direction, and I remember thinking, Is he talking to me? And then the guy behind me said "What, what?" because he thought Sammy was talking to him. It was hilarious.

As defending champion I played with Sammy the following year and there was so much security and so many carts you'd think I was playing with a sitting president. But what a special guy he was, and what an entertainer. He could do it all. They talk about baseball players who can do all five things: hit for average, hit for power, run fast, throw hard, and flash the leather. Well, that was Sammy as an entertainer. He could sing like crazy, dance with the best of them, play instruments, do impersonations, and act. And he loved golf as much as anything he did.

WHILE WE'RE NAME-DROPPING HERE, I had two days I'll never forget in the first two rounds of the 1995 British Open at St. Andrews. I was paired with Ernie Els, who was twenty-five and had won his first U.S. Open the previous summer, and Tiger Woods, who was just nineteen and playing off his exemption from winning his first U.S. Amateur the previous fall. I was forty-one and the grandpa in the group, but I had won twice earlier that year and was number three on the season money list. I told Fluff, "I think I'm paired with the future of golf right here."

Ernie played flawlessly the first two rounds. He was something like 10 under and held the thirty-six-hole lead. While Tiger and I were clearly in his wake, we both easily made the cut. I remember Ernie hitting nice low cuts and draws and working his ball beautifully in the windy conditions. Tiger, on the other hand, was hitting iron shots that would occasionally balloon up in the air. He was able to score well with his exceptional length off the tee and great touch around the greens, but he hadn't yet learned how to keep his ball down and work it both ways depending on the conditions of a particular hole.

I was on the range afterward, and Tiger came over to me and said, "Peter, I really enjoyed our round today, and I'd like to ask you a question. Is there anything you saw in my game out there that I could improve upon?"

It blew me away. Up to that point in my career, no other player had ever asked me anything like that. I told him, "Tiger, you know that when you play golf in Europe it's a totally different game than we play in America. In our country golf is played in the air. Over here, it's played on the ground." And then I talked about some of the shots that Ernie had played on various holes, how he used the wind as his friend rather than fighting it. I told him to watch Ernie on the range and observe how he was turning the ball down and knocking it under the wind, and taking more club and choking down on the grip to better control his ball flight. Tiger thanked me for the advice and went off to practice.

A little while later as I was walking to the putting green, Ernie stopped me and said, "Hey, Peter. Guess what happened? Tiger just walked up to me and asked me if I'd noticed anything in his game that he might improve." I told him the same thing had just happened to me, and we both gave each other this look, like Wow. Needless to say, we were impressed.

It should be mentioned that Tiger won the British Open at the same venerable St. Andrews course five years later by 8 shots, during his incredible 2000 season. Of course Ernie and I deserve all the credit for that, with the invaluable wisdom we imparted to him five years before. . . . *Not!*

As for Ernie Els, I think he's probably the most physically gifted player of our time. His combination of strength, magnificent touch, and a made-for-golf laid-back demeanor is the perfect package for a golfer. With some guys, their chili can run pretty hot and prevent them from getting the most from their games, but Ernie has a wonderful way of letting things that happen on the course float off his back. Oh, he gets concerned when he has a bad stretch of holes, but he's so talented that he knows he can always string together a bunch of birdies or eagles and get back into it. Early in the 2005 season, he was 8 strokes back going into the final round of the Sony Open in Hawaii, which he had won the previous two years, and he finished birdie, birdie, eagle on the last three holes for a course record 62 and missed getting in a playoff with Vijay by one stroke. That's talent. And that's confidence.

Sergio Garcia is another who has confidence by the truckload, and like his mentor Seve Ballesteros, he's fun to watch. Sergio has a brashness that borders on cockiness that turns off some people, but I admire him. I liked it a few years ago when he said his goal was to be the leading money winner on both the PGA and the European tours in the same year. It takes a lot of moxie to say that, and although he didn't back up his boast, it inspired him to play harder. The Tour needs all the spicy players we can get out there, and Lord knows we need more guys who are willing to share their true personalities.

Another guy who definitely has some zip is Hale Irwin. Here's a guy who turned sixty this past year, and he still has the spunk and drive of a rookie in his twenties, just starting out. As the 2005 season began, Hale had racked up forty Champions Tour victories, and eight Champions majors, to go with his twenty PGA Tour victories, which include three U.S. Opens. He is in his thirty-eighth season of playing full-time on the best tours in the world for which he was age-eligible. That's a remarkable record. You could argue that Hale's commitment to excellence is as strong as anyone's in the game. He would surely tell you that it takes a lot more effort and preparation to win at sixty than it did at fifty or forty, yet he's still willing to make the sacrifice and put in those hours in the gym and on the practice range well after a lot of guys would have retired to the back porch with the grandkids. And that's one of the things that makes golf such a great sport, the very fact that you can compete at a top level for four decades if you choose.

10

Tiger and Fluff . . . and Other Stuff

Speaking of Tiger Woods, I've got a story for you.

I first met Tiger in 1992 at the Los Angeles Open when he was sixteen years old. Tiger had won the U.S. Junior the previous summer and had been a recognizable name in golf circles for years, beginning with an appearance on television's *Mike Douglas Show* at the age of two in a putting contest with Bob Hope. He'd even been featured in *Golf Digest* magazine at the ripe old age of five.

Tiger was on the driving range at Riviera Country Club hitting balls with his father, Earl, watching, and I went up and introduced myself. I always try to do that with young players because I remember how important it was to me starting out when a veteran player went out of his way to make me feel comfortable. You never know for certain what path an outstanding junior golfer will follow, or whether he'll eventually make the PGA Tour, but if ever there was a sure thing it was Tiger. Skinny though he was then, he could absolutely crush the ball, and he was probably longer off the tee at that age than anyone but John Daly, and even that would have been a close call. He played at Riviera that week on a sponsor's exemption and missed the cut by a couple of strokes, but he still got all the buzz and everyone who watched him knew he was the real deal.

About a year later, I played in a pro-amateur shoot-out with him in the Western Open and got another look at his game up close. Tiger was paired with Tom Watson, who as a Stanford Cardinal would become a mentor to Tiger and help recruit him to his alma mater. My amateur partner was comedian Tom Dreesen, a great guy, but we were overmatched against the two TWs. Tiger was ripping it about 340 off the tee, and whipping wedges in there 2 feet from the hole, and I remember Dreesen saying wryly, "Gee, I don't know who Watson's celebrity partner is, but he's pretty good."

A few years later, during the U.S. Amateur at Portland's Pumpkin Ridge in late August 1996, I watched Tiger play a lot because I was taking a break from the Tour and rehabilitating a sore back. I followed him for several holes in the company of Nike founder and friend Phil Knight, who like me is a University of Oregon alum and with whom I'd had a professional relationship for years. Phil and his marketing people knew full well how much excitement and attention Tiger could bring to the game and the Nike Swoosh, and it came as no great surprise when they inked a huge endorsement deal with him soon after.

Of course, Tiger won his third straight Amateur that week in a thrilling playoff with Steve Scott. It was the sixth year in a row that he won a USGA national championship, a feat accomplished by only one other golfer, Bobby Jones. There was a lot of talk in the air about Tiger forgoing his final two years at Stanford and turning pro, and he'd already been offered several sponsors' exemptions to play in Tour events following the Amateur.

I had a conversation that week with Tiger, speculating about who he might get to caddie for him in those events.

"Why don't you use Mike Cowan?" I asked him. "Because I'm taking the next month off to rest my back, and Fluff is great. He's familiar with all the courses you'll be playing and will be a calming influence on you."

Tiger knew Fluff and liked him, and so we arranged it. It would keep Fluff employed while I was resting my back, and I thought it would be fun for my good friend to see this kid with such a great future in the game.

What I didn't know at the time was that Butch Harmon, Tiger's swing coach, had already contacted Fluff about that very possibility. So Mike Cowan was on the bag when Tiger made his debut at the Milwaukee Open, and I got several phone calls from both player and caddie during that week. I remember Tiger telling me how much he liked Mike, and that the other players were all being very friendly to him and he was having a great time. Tiger and I shared the same manager at the time, Hughes Norton with International Management Group (IMG), and I recall Hughes raving about Tiger and how poised and professional he was for someone just twenty years old. But the conversations I remember most vividly were with Fluff. In one of them he said, "Oh . . . my . . . God, Peter! This kid is a f—— machine! He is absolutely the greatest talent I have ever seen."

Fluff was totally blown away by Tiger, as both a player and a person. Woods's poise, intelligence, and professionalism were all things that Fluff raved about when we spoke. And these assessments were coming from a guy who'd seen it all in over twenty years on the Tour. Fluff had seen Palmer and Nicklaus and Johnny Miller and Tom Watson at the peak of their games, and here he was going on and on about a guy who was making his professional debut that week, calling him the best he'd ever seen. There was no way I couldn't be impressed by Fluff's comments about Tiger's talents. I was beginning to wonder if Fluff would throw up when he came back to watch me play my not-so-spectacular 280-yard drives and irons to the middle of greens.

Tiger made the cut easily at Milwaukee, but had a poor third round and finished only sixtieth. Nevertheless, he was all over ESPN *Sportscenter*'s highlight shows that week, scoring a dramatic hole in one on the 14th hole of the final round, and punching the air and emoting in a way that made for great television. If you took a poll among golfers and asked what they remember about the 1996 Milwaukee Open, I guarantee you more people would recall that it was Tiger's debut and that he made a hole in one than that Loren Roberts won the tournament.

The next week, in his second start, Woods finished eleventh in the Canadian Open, and he was just getting warmed up. The following week in Coal Valley, Illinois, at the Quad Cities Open, Tiger held the fifty-four-hole lead, one shot ahead of Ed Fiori, who at forty-three was old enough to be Tiger's father and who had been telling friends prior to that week that he planned to retire and become a charter-boat captain. Fiori was one of the shortest hitters on the Tour, hadn't won since the Bob Hope Desert Classic in 1982, and hadn't finished higher than 115th on the money list since 1989, and he was to be paired with Tiger in the final round. It was by any measure a total mismatch, except for the experience factor. Eddie knew how to win, and he's a gutsy competitor. Despite giving up 50 and 60 yards off the tee on every hole, Fiori beat Tiger by five shots head-to-head and won the tournament. Little did anyone realize then that it would take another seven years before anyone would overtake a Tiger Woods fifty-four-hole lead again.

The following week, Tiger finished third in the B.C. Open in Endicott, New York, in one of my favorite tournaments, and once again in my phone calls with Fluff he couldn't stop raving about Tiger and the incredible drives he was hitting and the imaginative shots he would pull off. After four weeks of watching the kid, it was clear that Fluff was beyond infatuated. He was head over heels in love with the golf game of Tiger Woods. Somewhere during this time, after hearing all of Fluff's anecdotes about Tiger's heroics, Jan said to him, "Mike, do you think you could caddie full-time for Tiger?"

And Mike said, "Oh, maybe, but I'm not prepared to leave Peter. That's not something I want to consider."

"Well, you should consider it," she said, "because that kid has an incredible future and it could be the opportunity of a lifetime for you. If that offer ever comes, you better take it."

Jan was basically saying what I was thinking, but I wasn't prepared to lose the guy who'd been by my side for my entire career as a professional. At that point in late 1996, I think Fluff and I had the longest running "marriage" on the Tour between caddie and player. As I wrote in *Buried Lies,* player-caddie partnerships have about the same longevity as Hollywood marriages. Anything lasting over five years is considered exceptional, and Fluff and I were on the verge of beginning our third decade together. We were the Paul Newman and Joanne Woodward of professional golf.

But this idea of Fluff moving on was something to be considered for another day, because the week after the B.C. Open I was returning to action at the Buick Challenge at Callaway Gardens in Georgia, and Fluff, as always, would be on the bag for me. Or so I thought until I got a phone call from him just as I was preparing to drive to the airport.

"I don't know how to say this, Peter," Mike said, "but I'm going to work for Tiger full-time. He offered me the opportunity of a lifetime, and I've got to take it. I'm sorry, you need to find another caddie this week. I'll be there with Tiger."

I felt like I'd been punched in the stomach. Although in hindsight I should have been preparing for this news, it hit me hard. I was being "fired" by my caddie, and it hurt. At that moment I felt the way Debbie Reynolds had when Eddie Fisher dumped her for Elizabeth Taylor. She could certainly understand that her man was going for someone who was better-looking, had bigger boobs, and was a much bigger star, but that didn't make it hurt any less. Here I'd done a favor by loaning my caddie out for a month, and without warning, a snatch-and-grab had taken place while I was back in Oregon mending my aching back.

In hindsight, I'm certain everyone realizes that it could have been handled much better, but it wasn't, and life goes on. Had Tiger and Butch and Mike made a conference call to me or sat down over breakfast and explained that Tiger and Fluff were a great match and if I were to give my permission, Tiger would want to hire Mike full-time, I would of course have agreed to part ways with him. It wouldn't have been easy, but I would have totally understood that it was the right situation for my friend. I learned later that Tiger had left a voice mail saying he wanted to discuss the caddie situation with me, but we never had a direct conversation about it.

Needless to say, the abrupt way it went down, with Fluff having to do the dirty work, didn't sit well with me at all. The phone calls from Tiger stopped cold at that point, and we went our separate ways.

I hired Scott Steele to caddie for me in Georgia, and then another weird thing happened. Tiger had committed to play that week, but before play began he withdrew, citing fatigue. I then got a call from Hughes Norton, who repped both Tiger and me, telling me that Tiger wanted me to go ahead and use Fluff that week, and then Fluff would pick up with him the following week. I wasn't about to fire Scott after I'd just hired him, so I declined the offer. At that moment I felt like a pawn in a chess game that I didn't know was even being played.

On reflection, the Tiger machine was moving pretty fast in

those first few months, the money surrounding it was enormous, and the whole structure of the PGA Tour was ramping up rapidly in dollars and visibility. TV ratings, fueled largely by Tiger, were exploding, and the television contracts—and with them the purses we were playing for—were going through the roof. In late 1996, I remember reading a column about the Holy Trinity surrounding Tiger Woods. There was Tiger's coach, Butch Harmon; his manager, Hughes Norton; and his caddie, Mike Cowan. Within two years, Mike and Hughes had been replaced, and by the end of 2002 Butch was gone as well. I guess when the flame burns that hot, anybody who gets too close can get scorched.

That week in Georgia was one of those horrible weather weeks where the tournament was called after thirty-six holes. I was proud that I played decently, a tie for twentieth, but it felt very odd to have someone other than Mike by my side. I definitely struggled with the separation, not only for the rest of that year, but all through 1997 as well.

The week following my "firing," I watched on television as Tiger won his first official PGA tournament, the Las Vegas Invitational. Although that's a tournament I had played in nearly every year, I elected to stay home that week. And while it was thrilling to watch Tiger come from four strokes back and win the playoff with Davis Love, and know that Fluff was part of the victory, it was definitely a bittersweet moment because I couldn't help feeling I'd been left behind. With Tiger's victory, figuring that Fluff was going to get the standard $1,000 per week plus 10 percent of the winner's purse, I realized that he was going to earn about $30,000 that week, which was more than he'd ever made in one tournament with me.

My coauthor Jack Sheehan is the master of ceremonies every year at the Las Vegas Invitational, and he gave me a full report in a phone call after the event. Jack said that in all the years he'd interviewed the winner on the 18th green, Tiger was the most composed champion he'd ever seen. Jack introduced him to the crowd as "the wealthiest college dropout in America." And Tiger's quick response was "Uh, I think Bill Gates has got me there." That savvy response would later be used in an American Express commercial.

And when Jack asked Tiger if he was surprised that he'd been able to win a PGA Tour event in just his fifth professional start, Tiger looked him dead in the eye and said, "To be honest with you, I'm surprised that it took this long."

Jack also told me that when he hugged Fluff and congratulated him on the win, Fluff said, "Give my best to Peter. I miss him."

Jack could see that Fluff was still very conflicted by what had transpired in the previous days and weeks.

IN ALL PROFESSIONAL ATHLETICS, when a guy comes along who changes the landscape of his particular sport, whether it's Muhammad Ali in boxing, or Michael Jordan in basketball, or Wayne Gretzky in hockey, or Tiger Woods in golf, people recognize the genius and the talent right away, and advisers and managers and personal assistants and eligible young women stumble all over one another to make sure they get in the good graces of the guy. It's simply human nature to want to bathe in that warm glow of celebrity and the perks that go with it. Who in the world could blame Mike Cowan for wanting to watch arguably the most talented guy ever to play golf from the best seat in the house?

It was interesting to watch Fluff's visibility increase, and the drama unfold, as the months went by. Fluff was part of one of the greatest moments in golf history when Tiger won the Masters by twelve strokes the following spring. When you consider that just twenty-five years before an African-American had never even been invited to compete at Augusta, and here was Tiger breaking the all-time scoring record and absolutely demolishing the best players in the world, well, I could only be excited for my friend that he was part of that historic occasion.

That season of 1997 produced a total of four victories for Tiger, with a record $2 million in official earnings, Player of the Year honors, and a host of other awards, not to mention constant visibility on the tube. Nike had paid Tiger a king's ransom in endorsement money to sport the company's Swoosh logo on his hat and clothing. Phil Knight and his brain trust rightly understood that the second most visible person to Tiger Woods on the PGA Tour was the man standing beside him as he hit all those heroic shots, so Fluff got a nice chunk of change as well. And because Tiger was so telegenic, and so dramatic in the way he played, the TV cameras were on him even when he wasn't in contention. You'd hear commentary that went something like this: "Here's Tiger on the thirteenth hole. He's eight strokes back but there's two par-fives and Sunday's round to play. He's done it before, so we wouldn't be surprised if he starts attacking every pin and begins to close ground."

Any excuse was used to aim the cameras at Tiger, and on the many weeks he chose to stay home and practice, the television ratings for golf took a nosedive.

I was also happy to see Fluff knocking down some great money. If you do some quick calculations and figure that Fluff made a thousand dollars a week for the twenty-one weeks Tiger played, and then on average 9 percent of the checks that Woods cashed, then Fluff made over $200,000 in 1997, not counting endorsement money, and he got plenty of that. Another way of looking at it is that Fluff earned enough on the course to easily rank in the top 125 money winners among the players.

It was really something to see my formerly reserved friend, who was basically an introverted guy in real life, start to emerge as a celebrity in his own right. In addition to his Nike deal, he was making commercials for Comfort Inns and a few other clients, and he was regularly being interviewed by the press about working for "the Man." The press needs material every day, and after they've gotten whatever they can from Tiger about his golf swing, his love life, his workout habits, and what video games he enjoys, then they want to know everything they can about his caddie. The world learned that Mike was a certified Deadhead who had attended well over one hundred Grateful Dead concerts and rated Jerry Garcia well above any golfers on his list of heroes. I'm sure the first time he started raving about his favorite lead singer to Tiger, Woods thought he was talking about Cherry Garcia ice cream from Ben & Jerry's. I knew there had to be a huge cultural generation gap between Tiger and Fluff, but hey, as long as Fluff could help him pull the right club and read greens accurately, and could understand his moods in the heat of battle, it didn't seem to matter that they were as different as night and day.

Did Fluff get caught up in his newfound celebrity? Of course he did, and I couldn't blame him. It's fun being recognized and treated like a hotshot. But Mike needed to keep his perspective about it, because a Tour caddie, while an important part of a team, is sort of like the lion handler in the days when the Christians and lions were in the arena. The caddie is part of the show, but he's not *the* show. And so it was an odd form of celebrity that Mike found himself wrapped up in, being the lead Sherpa for the most famous athlete in the world.

As the months progressed in 1997, I started to notice something unusual. It seemed that every time someone handed me a hat to autograph at a golf course, I would see Fluff's name in small letters up in the corner. I had never seen a caddie's autograph on anything, and I was seeing it all the time now, and I thought it was odd that it had gotten to the point that Fluff was signing as many autographs as top players like Greg Norman or Nick Price. Mike Cowan was the first caddie ever to sign autographs on a consistent basis.

I remember one time I saw Tiger and Mike walking to the range to practice and Tiger was engulfed with people and was signing stuff, and Mike was right behind him signing just as fast as Tiger. I remember telling Mike later that day that he shouldn't sign autographs while he was still on the clock. I said, "When you are done with work and walking to the car or in a restaurant by yourself or with other caddies, then it's cool to sign. But I wouldn't do it when you're with Tiger, because it makes you look like an equal, and the guy is still your boss."

Mike listened to what I said, and considered it, but he continued to sign autographs like it was no big deal.

I should explain something here about Mike Cowan's nickname. I have referred to him as Fluff in this chapter because that is how the public knows him. But I've always called him Mike . . . always. He got the nickname because in the mid-1970s, when he started out, he bore a resemblance to Steve Melnyk, a full-figured guy who was a Tour player then. Melnyk's nickname was Fluff, and Mike became known as "Short Fluff." Then when Melnyk quit playing and went to the broadcast booth, the "short" was dropped and the other caddies called Mike simply Fluff. But Mike never really liked the nickname, and during the years he caddied for me and started being recognized, when people in the gallery called out "Fluff," he would ignore them. It was only after he started caddying for Tiger that the press and public picked up on it, and the name was easy to remember and somehow made him more colorful.

Fluff had signed a few autographs as my caddie, especially after

I won twice in 1995 and made the U.S. Ryder Cup team. We had even done a couple of commercials together. A lot of people remember the one we filmed for Nike at the 17th hole at TPC Sawgrass, on the island green. By the magic of television, in the spot I make six or seven holes in one in a row and start walking across the water. We filmed it in the fall and the water was freezing. The producers had built a two-foot-wide Plexiglas walkway for me, just below the water's surface so I could do my best imitation of Jesus. (Needless to say, this was not typecasting.) And Fluff is walking two steps behind me and of course the idea is that, being a mere caddie, he hasn't quite perfected that walking-on-water routine, so he sinks into the pond and appears to drown, golf bag and all.

They put Mike in a Lycra wet suit under his caddie's jumpsuit, shirt, and slacks, and they did about twenty takes and he had to change clothes each time. I can tell you it wasn't pretty seeing Mike in that Lycra suit, which revealed every little bulge and wrinkle. He's not exactly cut like Lance Armstrong. Mike and I have that in common. Baggy—yes! Lycra—no! Anyway, I remember walking to the green during about the twelfth take and complaining about how slippery the Plexiglas was and how I felt like I might slip, and I heard Mike mumble under his breath, "You son of a bitch, you're worried about getting wet and I'm in this stinkin' water where fish f—— . . . freezin' my ass off. . . . Are they ready to wrap this f—— commercial yet, or what?"

So Mike was certainly well known among true golf fans when he went to work full-time for Tiger, but his Q rating went up a thousand percent after Tiger exploded on the scene. Throughout all that time, we remained in touch and spoke frequently, and he stayed close to Jan and our kids, who had always considered him like a favorite uncle. In fact, they always called him Uncle Mike. We had enjoyed too many great memories and wonderful times to let our relationship suffer.

HOWEVER, a little over two years after Fluff went with Tiger, I started to hear the drums beating in the distance. At the Los Angeles Open in 1999, Mike asked me to go to dinner with him. It was a Wednesday night, just before the tournament started, and he told me he thought he was going to get fired.

"Tiger didn't say a word to me today during the pro-am," he said.

And I said, "Ah, c'mon. Maybe he wasn't feeling well."

And he said, "Nah, he was interacting all day with his amateur partners. It was just me that he totally ignored. Not one word. He's acting like I'm invisible out there."

I had dinner with Mike again two nights later and nothing had changed. Tiger had made the cut and was actually in contention to win the tournament, but again he was totally ignoring Mike. And then Sunday night, after Tiger had finished second in the tournament, he didn't say a word to Mike.

"He just put his shit in his car and left," Mike said. "The entire week he didn't talk to me at all. I don't think there's any question that I'm toast."

A couple of days later, Mike's suspicions were confirmed when he got a phone call from Butch Harmon. Butch told him that Tiger appreciated all the good work he had done the last couple years, but that Tiger wouldn't be needing his services anymore. It had fallen on Butch to be the executioner, which was not the right way to handle matters, but that's the way it went down.

All the talk was that Tiger had fired Mike because he was signing so many autographs and doing commercials and that his newfound celebrity was getting in the way of his doing his job. But I think what it came down to was that Tiger and Mike were so different. There was that big age gap and culture gap and Tiger wanted someone a little closer to his age and a little more hip. Deep down, Mike is a salt-of-the-earth guy who can exist just fine with ten dollars in his pocket, and he has distinctly different tastes in music and food and culture, and I think Tiger just felt like he wanted a change at that time.

And so Tiger ended up with Steve Williams, who had worked for Greg Norman and Ray Floyd, and who in recent years has turned into an authoritarian type who once ripped a camera from a fan's hands and tossed it into a pond. It's quite a transition from mild-mannered Mike Cowan, but once again it's a partnership that has produced some great results, which shows that it's the player who is truly the celebrity and the one responsible for any fame that comes the caddie's way.

Mike wanted to come back and caddie for me at that point, and I certainly would have taken him back, but I had already hired a young man named Chris O'Connell, whom I liked very much, and I didn't want to drop the blade on Chris. It so happened that Jim Furyk, who was developing into a world-class player at that time, had recently fired his caddie, and so I talked to Jim and recommended he hire Mike. They are still together after six years. With Furyk, Mike has added a 2003 U.S. Open flag to his wall to go with his 1997 Masters flag. So all's well that ends well.

Although Tiger has won more than thirty golf tournaments and over $40 million since he fired Fluff, I don't think Mike frets over the fact that it could have been him on the bag through those years. He's appreciative of all that golf has given him, and continues to give him. After all, when he first started caddying for me in 1977 he was living in his car with a dog named Shivas and hoping just to earn food and gas money to get from one tournament to the next. The idea of being paid to act in television commercials was a long way from his mind.

Mike Cowan's career exemplifies just how far caddies have come in the last twenty-five or thirty years. In the 1970s, when not every round of every tournament was carried on some national television network, and most broadcasts included only the last four holes of the final two rounds, it is doubtful that the names or faces of any Tour caddies were known to casual golf fans. Oh, with his silver mane of hair and year-round tan, Angelo Argea, who caddied for Jack Nicklaus during his glory years, might have been familiar to a hard-core golf fan. And a few might have been able to identify Creamy Carolan, Arnie's caddie, or even Andy Martinez, who caddied for Johnny Miller in his prime and now loops for Tom Lehman. But other than two or three guys, no caddies were making any money at all. It was little more than a vagrant lifestyle for guys who didn't want to spend more than a week in one town before moving on.

Jack Sheehan recalls that when Dick Taylor, the late editor of *Golf World* magazine, hired him to write an article about his three-month stint as a Tour caddie in the early 1970s, just after Jack had completed his master's degree in English, Taylor said, "You are the first caddie I've ever met who can speak in complete sentences, pause at the commas, and stop at the periods."

Sheehan says that most of the caddies at that time traveled from one Tour stop to the next by car, usually four or five in a Volkswagen bus, and bunked in one room at Motel 6. "We didn't have any expectation of making any serious coin," Sheehan says. "Caddying was viewed as a great way to watch the best golfers in the world, see the country, and get some fresh air and exercise. The guys who made a career of it had very little education, not much in the way of family, liked the nomadic lifestyle, and simply figured that caddying was better than a real job. None of the guys who looped back then ever thought of caddying as a lucrative career. I agreed to caddie for a teammate from the University of Oregon, David Glenz, mainly because I couldn't find a teaching job."

I think often of some of the guys who were caddying when I started out. There was a fellow named Wingy, who was missing an arm; another named Adolphus Hull, who we called Golf Ball; and another we called "Down Wind Vic," because if you stood downwind from him the aroma was so strong you might start hallucinating.

Nowadays, there are probably as many as fifty full-time caddies on the PGA Tour who earn six-figure incomes. There are some fine young men like Scott Gneisser (David Toms), Joe LaCava (Fred Couples), John "Cubby" Burke (Davis Love III), and Jim "Bones" McKay (Phil Mickelson). They are bright young men, pretty good golfers in their own right, and the kind of guys who are making a great and lucrative career out there on the PGA Tour. They are the kind of people who could be successful in a variety of careers, but chose caddying because they love golf and can make a handsome living at it.

Throughout my career, I have spent nearly as much time in the company of caddies as I have players, because they are a fun and diverse group of individuals and they often have better stories to tell. They realize they are clearly second bananas in this traveling show, and because of that there's not an ounce of bullshit or pretense to them. I know if I ever get full of myself for even a second, the caddies on the PGA Tour will bring me right back to earth. And as Martha Stewart says, "That's a good thing."

11

Carrying On a "Tradition"

I've mentioned the Fred Meyer Challenge, the tournament we started in my hometown in 1986, sponsored by the Fred Meyer grocery chain. For seventeen years, it brought the best golfers in the world to Portland and became one of the most successful, if not *the* most successful, non-Tour events in golf. Over a million people attended the event through the years and over $13 million was raised for local charities.

Nicklaus, Palmer, Player, Trevino, Norman, Mickelson, Watson, Daly, and dozens of others came to Oregon each August for a fun, fan-friendly thirty-six-hole best-ball competition, and Peter Jacobsen Productions, which was originally formed to run the event, wanted to keep professional golf coming to our city. With the exception of two events played in Seattle in recent years, the Challenge was typically the only chance for golf fans in the Pacific Northwest to see the best players in the game.

As a result, it was more than disappointing when Fred Meyer, after being purchased by the Kroger Corporation, decided in 2002 not to continue its sponsorship. After a few minutes of moping, however, we picked ourselves right up and went out to find another sponsor.

Jeld-Wen, the world's largest manufacturer of energy-efficient windows and doors, based in Klamath Falls, Oregon, was interested in putting their name on a highly visible golf event, so I flew down to Klamath Falls to meet with them. The president and CEO, a man named Rod Wendt, was an avid golfer and a member of Waverly Country Club in Portland, and he surprised us by telling us he actually wanted to get behind something even bigger. Jeld-Wen didn't just want to sponsor an event—they wanted to sponsor a *PGA Tour event*.

There was an open spot on the 2003 PGA Tour schedule over Labor Day weekend, so we proposed an event called the Jeld-Wen Championship to be played in Portland. We filled out the paperwork and sent it to the Tour, thinking we had a done deal—and then found out that there were two other groups competing for the same dates, one headed by Greg Norman and the American Insurance Group, and the other by Tiger Woods. To no one's great surprise, Tiger's group got the event, and today it's the Deutsche Bank Championship, which is played at the Tournament Players Club of Boston. I understood the Tour's decision. Tiger has been the best and by far most visible player in the world almost from the day he hit the Tour in 1996, and to have him as the front man for a Tour event makes perfect sense. Commissioner Tim Finchem is right to engage Tiger in every way possible in the activities of the Tour, but that still didn't prevent Jeld-Wen from feeling like a jilted lover, as though they had been courted and left out in the cold.

About this same time, The Tradition, a Champions Tour major held at Desert Mountain in Scottsdale, lost its sponsor, and Jeld-Wen immediately seized the opportunity. Coincidentally, the dates we wanted were the same Labor Day weekend. Although we had short notice in which to put together a tournament for 2003, and the date fell just one month after the U.S. Women's Open played at Pumpkin Ridge in Portland, we staged a good tournament and had a wonderful result. Tom Watson won the inaugural Jeld-Wen Tradition with his great friend and longtime caddie Bruce Edwards on the bag. Everybody knew that Bruce was dying from ALS—it had been well chronicled when Tom led the U.S. Open after the first round six weeks before—and knew, too, it was very possible that The Tradition would be Bruce's last big win with Watson. Sadly, that turned out to be the case. Bruce died in April 2004, on the first day of the Masters, but I know the memory of that final big victory with him in Portland is very special to Tom.

The week was not without some controversy, however. I'll admit I was irked when Tom Kite complained every day to the media about the lack of attendance at the event. He didn't seem to appreciate that we had been scrambling for less than eight months to put the tournament together, and that we had accepted the event on short notice because we were confident that as long as we had our foot in the door, we could build it into something special. I got very tired of reading Kite's comments in the paper. It seemed to me that for Tom to be blasting this tournament that we'd saved from extinction, and that would certainly provide him some nice income, was like a restaurant owner blasting the food on his own menu. His criticism was not only inappropriate, it was downright shocking.

Please understand, Tom Kite is a good friend, but issues like this can boil up in the press and create tension on Tour. It happens in every family, and we work through them, but naturally I was sensitive to the criticism because we had worked so hard to bring the event to Portland.

When the Jeld-Wen Tradition returned in 2004, the situation was much improved. We would have the only major golf event in Portland that year, and I was eligible to play. Plus, I was coming off my win in the U.S. Senior Open the month before and I would be trying to win my second straight Champions Tour major. But it would not be easy. I would have a crazy schedule all week, wearing the two hats of competitor and tournament organizer.

From Monday morning of the tournament week until the seventy-two holes were finished on Sunday night, I would be going full bore. To give the reader an idea of what is involved in a week like that, let's go through it day by day.

Monday morning, Craig Stadler did a junior golf clinic for Nike, and Monday afternoon I played in the Nike Junior Shoot-Out. It was comprised of six Champions players and twelve juniors—six girls and six boys, high school champions from division I, II, and III schools in Oregon—playing in an alternate-shot format. It was a lot of fun and the type of event in which I love to participate, because the memories from that competition will last those kids a lifetime.

The junior event finished at about five-thirty and I immediately changed clothes and drove over to the Tiger Woods Building on the Nike campus in nearby Beaverton, where we were holding the Pro-Am Draw Party, hosted by Gulfstream. I emceed that event, which paired the amateurs for one round of competition with Champions Tour players. I got out of there about ten P.M.

Tuesday morning, I played in the pro-am, with an early tee time. Between doing media and some practice time on the range, I stayed at the course all day. Then I went to the Jeld-Wen skybox overlooking the 18th green and did two shows of *Peter and Friends* for the Golf Channel: a thirty-minute interview with Gary Player about his career, and a second show with Jim Thorpe, Pete Oakley, and D. A. Weibring, which was a roundtable discussion on what the Champions Tour meant to them. In Thorpe's case, what it meant was the ultimate mulligan, because he's made more money in the last five years than at any time in his life, and he's gone from what would be considered a solid player on the regular Tour to a superstar on the Champions Tour. With Pete Oakley, you had a club professional whose life and career totally changed when he won the Senior British Open. And with D.A., you had one of my best friends on the Tour, a guy who's done hundreds of clinics with me over the last twenty-five years, and who is a wonderful ambassador of the game. D.A. won five times on the PGA Tour and has already shown with a couple victories and regular appearances in the top ten that he's going to make a bundle of loot with the geezers.

After we did those shows on Tuesday I went to the Gulfstream Pro-Am Awards Party at the Hillsboro, Oregon, airport, where recording artist Edwin McCain entertained. We gave the winning pro-am teams a first-class trip to the Ketel One Vodka Ultimate Challenge Pro-Am at Dana Point, California, in November—a fun three-day golf vacation—and McCain was awesome. I really enjoyed myself, but I didn't get out of there until about ten-thirty that night. It had been a long day and my hip was stiff from standing too much, but I determined to do some stretching in the next day or two, and I was starting to put on my game face. After all, I wanted to win this major tournament in my hometown! With this schedule, though, it was going to be a tall order.

Wednesday morning, Jan and I got to the course early, and were guests on the *AM Northwest* show, on KATU channel 2 in Portland. The station is one of the founding sponsors of the event, and so we did about a ten-minute segment discussing such important matters as how I leave my underwear on the floor when I'm home. And my daughter Amy egged the show's hosts into revealing that she was upset that Taco Bell had recently removed Mexi-Nuggets from the menu. It wasn't exactly the *McLaughlin Report* or *Face the Nation* when it came to subject matter—just one of the dozens of things you're expected to do as a tournament host.

Although this was the official practice round, I didn't feel like walking eighteen holes. I know The Reserve golf course really well and have played it more than the other guys in the field, so I stayed around the range and did some serious practicing. At three-thirty, I hosted a clinic sponsored by American Containers, another major sponsor of the tournament, and I had Hale Irwin and D. A. Weibring with me. It was open to the public and about three hundred people showed up. There was some instruction, some Q-and-A, some humor, and shotmaking demonstrations, and I did some impressions of famous players. I have been doing them since I was about eight years old, initially to impress my mother and her friends, and later simply because they were fun to do.

Early in my career, my ability to do impressions and host clinics got me sponsors' invitations to certain events, which proved invaluable as I was scratching my way up the ladder on the Tour. Now I do them by popular demand. Some people think I could make a pretty good living just going around imitating Arnold Palmer pulling out chest hairs and throwing them up to test the direction of the wind, or pouring golf balls down my shirt and sliding my slacks down to show a half-moon in a Craig Stadler imitation. The impressions are sort of a blessing and a curse at the same time. They leave the indelible impression on golf fans that I'm just a screw-off jokemeister, but sometimes my back is hurting, and I just can't do them when I'm asked. But they do make people laugh every time, and there are few greater joys in life than entertaining people and lightening their load for an hour or two. So I still do them frequently, even with a bad hip, which is what I did on the Wednesday of the Jeld-Wen Tradition.

From there I drove back to the Tiger Woods Center on the Nike campus for the Champions dinner. This was for players only, and about fifty of the seventy-eight guys were there with their wives. Edwin McCain was there again, and I got up and sang McCain's hit "Let It Slide," which I bastardized into "Let It Slice," and Amy, our older daughter, who has a fabulous singing voice (*totally objective father here*), did a duet with him. It was a fun and relaxing night, but truthfully I was wiped out. I had been going nonstop since Monday morning. As we were driving home, I remarked that it felt like a Sunday night and that the tournament had just ended, but the truth was that we hadn't even put the peg in the ground for the first round. I had to get my mind straight and focus on four more days of important golf.

On Thursday morning, as we were about to tee off for the first round, I turned to my manager and sometimes caddie Mike O'Connell and said, "Man, I'm tired. Running the Fred Meyer Challenge was tough, but it was just two days. This is *seven*."

I don't remember ever standing on the first tee of any tournament and complaining about being tired. Normally, I'm totally pumped up and excited to get out there and make some birdies. The first tee is typically a place where I have to force myself to calm down, but this was a distinctly different experience.

I was paired with Isao Aoki, who is a great guy, but that meant there wouldn't be a lot of conversation during the round, because Isao speaks only about twenty words of English, which is about the same as me with Japanese. I knew whatever I said to him, or any joking around I would do, would be received with a big smile, a polite "Thank you very much," and some bowing. Despite being tired, I was swinging well enough that I managed to get around on Thursday in a respectable 69, 3 under par and two back of the lead.

Following the round, I did some media interviews and then stayed and practiced for a while. There was no point in going home because I was scheduled to host a players' forum that night in a public tent near the 18th green. It was called the Cheerful 19th

Hole, and the venue had Golden Tee video games, and there was food and booze. The players' forum is strictly for the fans, to let them get to know the players and learn more about the Champions Tour. I hosted the panel and my guests were Bruce Fleisher, Ben Crenshaw, and Allen Doyle.

Too often, when you ask players to do things like this, something beyond their normal play and practice routine, you get responses like "Do you really need me?" And if they agree to do it, they'll sometimes come up an hour before and say, "Are you sure I need to stick around for that deal? Is it still happening?" But invariably once it's done, they thank me and say, "Hey, that was a good time. I'm glad I did it." And such was the case that night. Bruce Fleisher had been labeled a can't-miss star after he won the U.S. Amateur and several other big amateur events about thirty-five years ago, but had had a sporadic PGA Tour career, with many injuries and several stints as a club pro interrupting his competitive life. Once he turned fifty, however, and hit the Champions Tour, Fleisher became a dominant player. He has proven time and again that he can hang with the likes of Irwin and Kite, who had Hall of Fame careers on the PGA Tour. So Bruce couldn't be more grateful for the mulligan the Champions Tour has afforded him, and he'll explain that to the public every chance he gets.

Allen Doyle is another guy with an interesting story, because of his unorthodox short swing, and the fact that he was essentially unknown until he came out and won a flock of tournaments once he turned fifty. Allen played hockey growing up, and was an outstanding amateur golfer, but he didn't turn professional until he was forty-six. He did so strictly because he felt he could make a go of it on the Champions Tour. And he's been one of the most consistent players out here over the last six seasons. He is so excited to be making a fabulous living, and he shares that excitement every time he does an interview. He fully appreciates that twenty-five years ago that opportunity just wasn't available to a talented golfer hitting the half-century mark.

And of course golfers love Ben Crenshaw as much as any player in the modern era. He took questions that night about his two wins in the Masters, his amazing captaincy of the dramatic U.S. Ryder Cup victory in 1999, and his career as a golf course architect. The people absolutely loved it. It's the type of thing we need to do more often, and since the Champions Tour has become more fan-friendly in recent years, the public response has been terrific. From the fairway interviews during play, to the player interviews on the couch, this Tour can grow and thrive only by reaching out to the fans in every regard.

When the forum was finished on Thursday evening at about seven-thirty, Jan and I left the course and stopped at a restaurant for dinner. As we were driving home, the sun was still up and I felt like it was the first relaxing moment I had enjoyed all week. After dinner, I chipped and putted in the backyard for a while, which is my way of unwinding while still feeling like I'm accomplishing something, and watched some television. I didn't tee off the next day until about twelve-thirty.

Friday morning, I caught up on my stretching, which was critical to keeping my hip loose. At the U.S. Senior Open, I had been responsible about doing everything necessary to keep my hip, legs, and back in shape, but my responsibilities at home in Portland made it nearly impossible to stay on the same regimen. Partly because I felt so good, I went out Friday and had a terrific round. I hit every fairway and every green and shot 66. It was one of my best ball-striking rounds in a long time. I really didn't make any putts to speak of, just cleaned up on short birdie putts and par 5s. I had a one-shot lead after thirty-six holes, and the guys on the Golf Channel seemed to be in agreement that it was my tournament to lose.

I did some interviews after the round, but unlike in the Senior

Open, where I was leading after thirty-six holes and just praying my hip would hold up long enough so I could finish the tournament, in the Portland media sessions I expressed a lot of confidence in my ball-striking. More than anything, I talked about how delighted I was with the large galleries and how smoothly the tournament was running.

I've always felt that professional golfers do as well or better in media interviews than any other professional athletes. The game teaches you good manners and etiquette, and the ability to comport yourself well on a one-on-one basis with fellow players. In most other sports some big-name athletes act like they're doing reporters a big favor when they sit for an interview or show up at a press conference. But watch Phil Mickelson sometime, or Ernie Els or Davis Love. They not only offer good answers, but they can be fascinating to listen to. They'll talk at length about their thought process on the course, what things they're working on in their swings, and the pressures and rewards the game gives them. I believe so much of the poise of present-day players comes from the example set by Palmer, Player, Nicklaus, Trevino, and Ray Floyd, the guys the current generation watched as they were coming through the ranks. About 99 percent of the time, the men and women in the media will give you a fair shake if you respect that they are doing their jobs the same way we players are, and so I look at press conferences or one-on-one interviews as a valuable conduit to getting our message or story out to the public. Press interviews are a privilege. We don't need to worry about the media or what they might want to know until they *stop* asking questions or caring what we have to say.

So Friday evening, I got home about eight o'clock, and I wasn't scheduled to tee off Saturday until about two P.M. This is the odd part about playing a tournament in your hometown and sleeping in your own bed. When you have that much time on your hands, you have no idea what to do with it. I got up at seven-thirty and turned on the tube. I watched Scooby-Doo for a while, but quickly got bored with that and had the thought that I could clean the garage. So I sat down until that idea went away.

And then I thought, No, I'll clean out my closet. I quickly de-prioritized that idea as well, and decided instead to go into my den and write some thank-you notes for the letters and phone calls I had gotten after the U.S. Senior Open. I was getting started on that when, all of a sudden, I stopped myself and said, Oh my God. I'm playing today. I'm leading the tournament. Because I was in my own home and was so comfortable, for about an hour I had forgotten about it, which was both a good and a bad thing. It was good because my mind was off my golf game, but then I realized I had to get it back on my game, which was hard to do because it had been at least twenty-five years since I had led a medal play golf tournament while staying under my own roof. The last time was at the Oregon Open in 1978, shortly after I joined the Tour. I had been able to hang on that year and edge out my brother-in-law Mike Davis, Jan's older brother. So I came to grips with the reality that I was at home, and leading a Champions Tour major that I wanted to win badly. I had already told the media that I was donating whatever money I won to the tournament's charitable foundation, and I just couldn't wait to turn over the $360,000 winner's check to them. What a neat payback that would be for everyone who helped bring big-time golf back to Portland.

To further elaborate how different it is to be leading a tournament at home rather than on the road, let me tell you what I did in a similar situation the month before at the U.S. Senior Open in St. Louis. In Missouri, I would get up early, watch ESPN's *Sportscenter* until I knew the previous day's scores and results so well I could have passed a multiple-choice exam about them. Then I'd go down to the workout room and ride the bike and stretch for a while, then return to my room, read the newspaper, watch *Sportscenter* again to make sure I hadn't missed anything, then check out the Golf Channel to see how sweaty I looked on the film clips.

At home I found myself just watching the minutes pass slowly by, going stir-crazy. After what seemed like days, it finally got to be noon and I headed out to play the third round with Bruce Lietzke. Round three was unusual in that it went almost perfectly for the first ten holes. I then missed the 11th green short left, had an extremely difficult little pitch out of heavy grass and over a mound, and darned if I didn't pitch it in for another birdie. I was 13 under par, and knew I was leading, but I wouldn't learn until later that I had a four-stroke lead at that point. I was definitely in control of the tournament, in my hometown, on a course I knew better than anyone in the field. And wouldn't you know it, just when things looked like they were going so well for me, my putter went into the deep freeze. From the 12th hole to the house, I hit some great iron shots, had numerous close birdie chances, but made absolutely nothing and compounded the cold spell with a bogey on the 17th hole. My lead went from four strokes to zero in little over an hour. And maybe that's what makes this crazy game so intriguing. You can never take anything for granted, even for a second, and golf is much like life in that the minute you feel on top you are likely to have your legs knocked out from under you.

There are so many different ways of dealing with adversity. I'm pretty pragmatic about it, but other players have their own methods. Craig Stadler, for instance, approaches bad breaks under pressure, or lipped-out putts, as though they don't matter, almost like he's given up and to heck with it. He acts like the neighborhood grouch after the rascally neighbor kids have just sprinted across his yard, picked apples off the tree, and thrown him a moon as they ran off. It's like he's thinking, Damn bleepin' kids. And so Stads will kick his bag, flip his club to his caddie, and act like he hates life and that he's resigned to how difficult it is. When a putt misses, it's like he expected it, that it always happens to him, and that it doesn't really matter because life is just a big ol' shit sandwich. In an odd way, when Craig does that, it takes the pressure off him. What that behavior allows Stadler to do is actually stay in the moment and focus on the little picture rather than getting carried away with the big picture. I don't know how many times I've seen Craig act like he's raised the surrender flag—that the tournament just doesn't mean squat to him anymore—and by removing the burden of feeling like he's in contention he hits wonderfully tension-free shots on the ensuing holes and starts making birdies again. Little did I know then that the same thing was going to happen during the final round Sunday.

I HAD THE SAME DILEMMA Sunday morning that I'd had on Saturday. I was home, figuring out a million ways to be productive around the house, but was eager to get to the course and start the final round. But again I had the last tee time, at two P.M., with Vicente Fernandez from Argentina. We were tied for the lead, with a large posse right on our heels. It was certain to be an exciting final day for the Portland fans, and never in my career had I felt a crowd pulling harder for me than on that day. And that creates its own kind of pressure. A few weeks later, I saw Mike Weir face that same kind of responsibility when he was leading the Canadian Open coming down the stretch. No Canadian golfer had won his national open in fifty years, and it didn't happen that day, either. Even though Mike had a three-shot lead with seven holes to go, Vijay Singh was able to catch him and beat him in a playoff. You could see the stress etched on Mike's face the entire back nine, as tens of thousands of Canadians were screaming for him to pull it off. Vijay, meanwhile, was just whistling along, knowing he had just claimed the number-one spot in the world ranking the week before with his sixth victory of the season, and that winning in Canada would just add more icing to his cake. I don't care how great a champion a player is, the urgency of wanting to win in front of a home crowd is intense and can cloud your thinking.

Back to the final round of the Jeld-Wen Tradition. After bouncing around the house for four or five hours, doing some e-mails, writing a couple songs, rotating the tires on the SUV, simonizing the interior of my wife's Lexus, and partaking in a meditation session with my sensei (yeah right!), I headed to the course. I felt good, had a high level of confidence, and had every intention of allowing the crowd support to lift me up, not create more pressure.

I piped a drive on the 1st hole, and hit a sand wedge in there about 15 feet below the hole. I hit a good putt, which burned the edge and went by about 16 inches. In every Saturday morning two-dollar Nassau in America, the putt was a gimme. It was one of those "Pick it up, Fred, it's early and we'd hate to see you make a fool of yourself on the first hole" type of putts. But obviously, we have to hole 'em all in the big leagues. Before I cleaned it up, Vicente knocked in a nice birdie putt, so he was one ahead. As I was standing over my little one, I noticed that there was a tournament marshal standing in the middle of the fairway, right in front of the green, in my line of sight behind the hole. It's never a group of people that will distract you, but always the one individual, because you're wondering whether he's going to do jumping jacks, hold up a verse from Scripture, or just turn and walk away while you're putting. I motioned for him to move to the side, but couldn't help but wonder why he was standing there while I was putting. And this is where my operations hat went on over my player's hat. Why was a tournament volunteer, *our* tournament volunteer, standing right in front of the green when he should know better? That thought took my mind off the putt and I missed it. Of course

it was my fault, I could have moved him entirely away, but I figured from 16 inches I could still kick it in. I immediately walked
over to him after missing it and nicely asked him why he was there.
He said, "Oh, I'm collecting the pins, Peter." That's something
that's always done after the last group has putted out, so spectators
don't steal the pins for souvenirs. But normally someone assigned
this task waits until the final group has left the green and moved to
the next tee. I was kinda mumbling to myself all the way to the
next tee about how we need to give better instructions to our volunteers, but the incident forced me to refocus and become more
determined to hit positive shots and not dwell on mistakes.

I did a good job of it, staying in the present tense, but I still
wasn't making any putts. The story of the first eleven holes was
that I'd hit a good drive, hit an approach shot in there 10 to 12 feet,
burn the lip on the putt, and tap in for par. It's what I had done all
week. Finally, on the 12th hole, I hit a sand wedge a foot from the
hole for a tap-in birdie to put me one stroke back of the lead, and I
thought, Here we go. At that point I was 11 under par for the tournament and there were about ten guys sniffing the lead. I don't remember at that point seeing Craig Stadler's name anywhere on the
board. I then parred the next three holes to stay in the picture, but
noticed that Jerry Pate had gotten to minus 14 with just two holes
to go. He had holed an iron from the fairway on number 16 for eagle, and looked like he was going to grab his first professional victory in over twenty years. Here was a guy who, early in his career,
looked like a sure-thing Hall of Famer. He won the U.S. Open at
just twenty-two years of age, and seven more tournaments before
injuries basically shelved his career. And now the Champions Tour
had given him a second chance to show his talent. When I saw
Jerry's name on top, several quick thoughts went through my
head. I thought how cool for Jerry and his wife, Soozi, if he won
the tournament, a major, and what a great comeback story that

would be. But of course I was also out there competing, so the fighter in me thought, Wow, I have to get on my horse to get to 14 under.

I figured I surely needed to birdie the two par 5s, 16 and 18, to have any chance to win or get in a playoff. I hit a good drive on the 16th and had 235 yards to the pin, which was cut in the back right corner of the green. The 16th is a huge green with an awkward back right quadrant that's not really big enough for a pin position. It is not the kind of green I would ever design, but that's what I was faced with. I hit a good five-wood right at it, but it scooted to the back fringe and left me a tough chip. I executed it pretty well, but left myself a curling 5-footer for birdie. At that point, Pate was struggling to get to the clubhouse, and the birdie would put me 13 under, in good shape. But once again my putter failed me, and the crowd let out a big groan. Still, going to the tough 17th, a really good long par 4, I was at 12 under, and I noticed that Craig Stadler was alone in the clubhouse at minus 13, and I remember thinking: How the hell did Stadler get there? I hadn't seen his name all day, and then suddenly there he was on top.

While the 17th hole normally plays about 465 yards, the tee was forward on Sunday so that it was only 420. Normally I hit a driver there, but I felt I could draw a three-wood down the fairway far enough to have an eight- or nine-iron in. I absolutely nutted the tee shot and quickly picked up the tee. It was just the shot I wanted, but then I noticed that the ball was turning left a little more than I'd expected, and then it took a hot bounce left from there. That really surprised me, because the fairways were wet and most tee shots plugged or just took one bounce when they landed.

As I approached the landing area, I was again surprised to see no ball there, and then I saw people in the gallery pointing at the edge of the creek. My ball had ended up on a steep, 45-degree bank. It was a really bad break, but surprisingly the ball was sitting up perfectly. The lie reminded me of Fred Couples's ball sitting on the front bank of the 12th hole at Augusta National when he won the Masters in 1992. I mean I couldn't believe a ball on that steep an angle could sit up that nicely. I said to my caddie, "Mike, I can hit that ball. I really think I can hit that ball."

I was not only trying to convince Mike, I was really trying to convince myself. He looked at me as though I'd told him I thought we should find some sawed-off shotguns and knock off a savings and loan on the way home. But he didn't say anything. He just watched me thinking my way through this mess. I had 143 yards to the hole, and if I executed the shot, it was possible to knock the ball on the green. The odds were against me, no question, but it was possible. I felt I had to make par-birdie on the last two holes to have a chance for a playoff, and there was even that positive thinking part of me that said I could knock this shot on the green, hole the putt, and make a bid for "Shot of the Day" on the Golf Channel.

I took off my socks, put my golf shoes back on over my bare feet, skittered down that bank like a land crab and waded into the creek. The water was up to my knees, and I had to be careful not to break any rules by building a stance in a hazard. I actually called over an official and explained everything that I was doing so I wouldn't get a penalty. In the creek, my feet sucked down into the mud about four inches. Literally and figuratively, I was ankle-deep in shit. Understand, the average golfer couldn't even hit the ball and would probably fall backward into the water if he took a swing in that predicament, but having played the game competitively for forty years, I've encountered every situation imaginable, and part of what we do every day as professional golfers making a good living at this game is to attempt difficult shots and pull them off. In hindsight, in this particular case perhaps the natural optimism that was responsible for any success I've had in my career outweighed pragmatism. I wanted to win this tournament so badly, and I was so eager to turn over that first prize of $360,000 to the tournament charities, that I tried a shot I shouldn't have. The result was disastrous. With my baseball swing, I hit the ground about an inch behind the ball, which flattened out the club and smothered the club face, and the ball went dead left into the water. Oh, the shot got on *Sportscenter* that night all right, but with a lot of groaning in the background and a lot of "What was he thinking?" from the broadcast booth.

I didn't lose my cool, although the shock of knowing I'd lost the tournament right there hit me immediately. And I even had a moment of clarity as I was toweling off and putting my dry socks back on, that despite this sudden disappointment, it had still been a great week because I'd been in contention the entire way, we had drawn some good crowds out to watch the tournament, and the event had been successful for Jeld-Wen and the Portland community. I finished the hole by making a double bogey 6 and then birdied the final hole to finish in a logjam, tied for fourth at 11 under. Craig Stadler, who had been totally out of the tournament at 8 under par after thirteen holes, birdied the last five to edge Jerry Pate and Allen Doyle by one shot. A friend in the gallery told me Stadler had acted like he'd totally surrendered the ship after the 13th hole, but once again Craig's odd way of handling adversity had landed him in the winner's circle. The finish made for fine drama, as no fewer than eleven guys had a chance to win in the last hour of play. I can never remember a time when that many guys had a shot that late in the game.

Make no mistake. After doing the media interviews and hearing that there was a ton of second-guessing of my decision on number 17, I was feeling pretty low. Forget the fact that all the broadcasters were second-guessing me; hell, I was second-guessing myself.

I'll admit that I even cried a little on the drive home. Maybe that shows how much I still care, but the emotion was there mainly because I wanted to win so badly in my hometown. Nevertheless, I was able to donate a fat check to deserving charities, and I know that money was put to good use.

I was totally exhausted Sunday evening, and wanted nothing more than to crash for about eighteen hours, but I had to catch a flight to Lake Tahoe for an outing the next day at the opening of a new Jack Nicklaus golf course.

The pain of the bad finish would erode in a few days. A great aspect of my life as a professional golfer is that redemption is always as close as the next tee.

12

Things We Can Do Better

No ONE'S EVER CALLED me shy about expressing my opinions. I'm sure there are some people who'd love to shut me up! But I'd like to close this book by talking about some of the things we do well in professional golf—and things we could do better.

One of the wonderful benefits of winning the Greater Hartford Open in 2003 was that it gave me a return ticket to the Mercedes Championships at Kapalua on Maui in 2004. I played pretty well, nothing spectacular, and finished smack dab in the middle of the pack. My tie for fifteenth earned me a check for just over $89,000, which was far more than I had banked in any of my first three victories on Tour. Thanks again, Tiger.

There was one thing disappointing about the Mercedes Championships, however, and it was that the tournament dispensed with some of the traditions that had made the event special in the past. They used to gather together all of the players at a mandatory cocktail party or dinner and take a group photograph of all thirty of us, the guys who had won one event or more the previous year. They didn't do it this time. It would have been a nice picture to look back on when I'm seventy, to recall that I competed in a special field with Tiger Woods and Vijay Singh and Phil Mickelson and all those great players. Traditions are hard to develop and easy to forget. When the Tournament of Champions first started in the 1950s at the Desert Inn Country Club in Las Vegas, there used to be a talent show for the players—Sam Snead played the trumpet, Gary Player did a soft shoe, and the Hebert brothers, Lionel and Jay, performed as a singing duet. Now, how cool is that tradition? I would give my left Titleist to have gotten up there at Kapalua with my guitar and cranked out a few tunes, and maybe watched Tiger doing his skit where he bounces a ball on a club and whacks it off a chandelier in a ballroom. That talent show made the tournament even more special, but it somehow got lost through the years. It's a shame because I'm sure it brought the players closer together and gave them something to rib each other about for the next twelve months. Not to mention the photo opportunities.

In 2004 and 2005, Matt Griesser and I volunteered to host the draw party at the Sony Open, just to add a little spice to what can be a dreadfully boring evening. In 2004, for the benefit of the amateurs, we read off a list of "Pro-Am Do's and Don'ts." For example, one was "If you happen to skull your Heaven-wood from 132 yards up there three feet from the hole and you're all excited because your fat handicap allows you two strokes on the hole, don't turn to your pro and say, 'Okay, pro, I want you inside of me,' because the comment could be taken the wrong way."

So in 2005 we decided to borrow from David Letterman and do a couple of Top-Five lists. The first list we read was: *The Top Five Signs That You Are Going to Have a Really Good Pro-Am Experience.*

Number 5: After your opening tee shot, Ernie Els asks if he can try out your driver on the next tee.

Number 4: On the seventh green, Tom Lehman asks you to be his assistant captain for the 2006 U.S. Ryder Cup team.

Number 3: The cart girl asks how long you've been playing on the Tour.

Number 2: You actually get a smile out of Craig Stadler.

And the Number 1 reason you know you're going to have a really good pro-am experience: Michelle Wie asks you to escort her to her junior high cotillion.

And then we did *The Top Five Signs That You Are Going to Have a Tough Day in the Pro-Am.*

Number 5: Every shot you hit, your pro says, "Nice out."

Number 4: The only way you help your team all day is by paying for the hot dogs and sodas at the turn.

Number 3. Your pro calls the PGA Tour official over to see if they haven't inadvertently dropped maybe one or two zeroes off your handicap.

Number 2: You spend most of the day trying to convince your pro that those really were practice swings.

And the Number 1 sign that you are going to have a tough day in the pro-am: Your pro asks you to pick up for the third time . . . on the same hole.

We got a great response to these lists from the amateurs, probably because they hit so close to home.

The night was topped off by the showing of the new Sony film *Hitch,* which hadn't been released yet, and the appearance of the two stars, Will Smith and Kevin James. Those guys actively participated in the draw party, with Will announcing that Kevin's 12 handicap was an absolute fraud, because Kevin had hit a 320-yard drive in the practice round that day. Will suggested we do a simple test on Kevin . . . a urine test. Everybody laughed, and I said to Will, "Okay, we are going to do just that, and I'm putting you in charge of obtaining that sample." And on cue Griesser turned around and acted like he was unzipping his pants and I got down on my knees like I was holding the piss bottle. This wasn't what you call highbrow humor, but it pumped some laughter into the evening and the amateurs had a great time with it. There's no reason that something funny and different can't be done every week for the amateurs to enhance their whole experience playing in programs.

ANOTHER THING that has changed dramatically in the last decade is that there isn't nearly as much camaraderie on Tour. I think it's a dangerous trend. It so happens that a lot of our top players today are introverts, or at least they've trained themselves to become introverted because they feel they need to do that to play well. They not only don't hang out much with other players; worse, they don't feel any responsibility to hang with the corporate sponsors and the people who are directly responsible for providing our Tour with its gargantuan purses. I'd certainly be kidding myself if I said that in 2003, at the age of forty-nine, I was a better golfer than I was at thirty or thirty-five or forty, and yet primarily because I won one tournament in the days when the average purse is about $5 million, and the winner bags somewhere between $800,000 and a million, I earned more official money in '03 than in any of my previous twenty-eight years on Tour. And because I'm grateful for the living I'm able to make playing a game I love, I feel a tremendous responsibility to interact with the people who make this income possible.

I have strong opinions about why the younger players have become so withdrawn. I'm afraid they've taken Tiger Woods's success and popularity for granted. Everything just exploded when Tiger came on the scene in the fall of 1996. He was the most celebrated amateur to turn pro since Jack Nicklaus some thirty-five years before. With his amazing power, good looks, telegenic charisma, athletic demeanor, and ability to draw minorities to the game, Tiger hit the Tour as the perfect specimen to boost national and international interest in professional golf. Then when he won the Masters by twelve strokes just seven months after turning professional, and in the process broke Nicklaus's longtime Augusta scoring record, the world understandably fell in love with him. Every talented young player on the planet wanted to act like Tiger, swing like Tiger, and get buff like Tiger. For the first time ever, golfers hit the gyms and weight rooms en masse. The new number-one player had raised the bar a clear notch higher for anyone aspiring to be the best in the sport.

The young guys also saw that being like Tiger was going to take a little selfishness. After all, he was single, totally focused on the goal of becoming the greatest player ever, and had surrounded himself with a team of handlers and managers who deflected as many distractions as they could. Although he could be a lively interview subject, after he felt he was burned by a *GQ* magazine interview in which a reporter repeated some offhanded jokes from Tiger that were not intended for public consumption, Tiger quickly became guarded around the media. I'm not being critical of Tiger. God knows he's given back wonderfully to the sport in ways that it would take an entire chapter to document. It's just that he quickly became the gold standard for the sport, and that was interpreted by many of the guys coming up as the way they had to handle themselves if they were going to stay anywhere in his wake. As a result, an important aspect of the Tour—being friendly and personable with corporate sponsors and volunteers, and providing lively, fun, and honest interviews for the media—got pretty much put on the back shelf as a low-priority item.

In 1976, when I first joined the PGA Tour, Arnold was still the King, and Nicklaus, Johnny Miller, and Tom Watson were the dominant players. The field of battle for the PGA Tour was comprised of players, caddies, ropes and stakes, spectators, an occasional bleacher, and a Porta Crapper every fourth hole. Over the past twenty years, however, tournaments have morphed into civic happenings. Tournament sites are now corporate villages. The Ryder Cup is no longer just a biennial competition between Europe and the United States that nobody would ever go to because the U.S. was so dominant. It's now a huge television ratings success, and getting a ticket is about as hard as getting into the Academy Awards. All that's largely because the top echelon of the sport has become a corporate bonanza for companies that see professional golf as a great way to sell their products and define their image.

The Ryder Cup and major championships like the British Open and U.S. Open actually set up their own little cities where companies entertain clients and tout their products. Even regular Tour events can have as many as twenty corporate hospitality suites or chalets on the golf course, where social activities go on all week. The PGA Tour is all about corporate marriages. Anheuser-Busch/ Michelob is the official beer, Coca-Cola is the official soft drink, National car rental is the official ride. These companies love golf and admire the players, and so it just makes sense that the players should spend a little part of each day giving something back to them. To return the love, so to speak.

We ensured that this happened at the Fred Meyer Challenge when we hosted it in Portland. The way we did it was to assign a host to each player. For instance, I would have my brother David host Arnold Palmer. David would escort Arnold, as soon as he walked off the 18th green and signed his scorecard, up to the Fred Meyer corporate tent to mingle with the executives there, and after that take him next door to the UPS tent. The execs and their guests would have a few pictures taken, and Arnold would maybe grab a snack and a Coke and sign a couple of autographs. Then David would walk Arnold down to the locker room. It might take twenty to thirty minutes, but those little gestures would do wonders to solidify our relationship with our sponsors, and it would be that small interaction that would be most savored by the guests, long after talk about the golf was over.

It just seems like this sort of payback to sponsors and volunteers and fans is the right thing to do, in every sense, and yet we fail to do enough of it on the PGA Tour. The players typically go straight from the 18th green to the driving range or fitness trailer or get on the phone with their swing guru to analyze their thought process during the just-completed round, because they are convinced that is what they need to do to get to the top. There is a serious loss of perspective there.

As Jackie Burke once told me in an interview for ABC television, "Yeah, Jimmy Demaret and I had a golf psychologist. His name was Jack Daniel's. And we'd visit him in the bar after nearly every round." (By the way, both Demaret and Burke are in the World Golf Hall of Fame.)

I feel strongly that the Tour needs to gear its marketing of our product with a greater emphasis on player involvement with the sponsors and volunteers and people who make our profession so successful.

While I've said that, I do think the PGA Tour has the best image of all professional sports when it comes to having quality guys of good character. You just don't read stories of our guys getting into scrapes, maybe with the exception of John Daly, and even he has overcome that by being so good with the fans. John will sign autographs until his hand drops off, and people kind of view him as the one fallible everyman-type character on the Tour, and so they forgive him nearly all his transgressions.

I can tell you that when the red light of television isn't on them, so many of these young guys who come across as flatliners are really warm, fun guys in the locker room. I just wish they'd express it more in public, and make that extra effort to ingratiate the major boosters and corporate bankrollers behind the game. I can't tell you how often I hear an amateur say something like, "You know, I played with So-and-so today, and even though he doesn't show it on TV, he's really a great guy with a dry sense of humor." I just wish the guys on Tour would trust their natural personalities more in the public eye.

The essence of my point is that while Tiger has it all, other players who try to emulate him may have only a part of it. Tiger can decide not to do an interview or go to the press room after a round, and the public will look past it because he was so darned much fun to watch on the golf course. Fans are on the edge of their seats constantly because they just never know when the next shot he pulls off will be one that will make highlight reels for the next ten years. And the Tiger of 2005, compared to his rookie year, gives a hell of an interview. He's bright and witty, but if a reporter asks a stupid question he's liable to have a verbage burger shoved down his throat, so in that sense he keeps the journalists on their toes as well.

When I watch some of the younger players give interviews after a round, I wish the public could hear them describe the same shot in the locker room. They might have to hit the bleep button a few times, but it would be fun.

Here's an imaginary interview of a relatively unknown player who's taken the first-round lead at Quad Cities with a 64. See if it doesn't sound familiar:

ANNOUNCER: Great round today, Ronnie.
RONNIE: My name's Ron.
ANNOUNCER: Oh, sorry, uh, Ron. Tell us about those eight
    birdies. You really had that putter working.
RON: Yeah, I got a good feel for the speed of the greens. My
    stroke felt good. This Penncross Bent 319 with rye over-

seed really fits my eye. Plus, I've been working a lot with Dave Pelz and my golf psychologist. I try to think of the hole as being half full rather than half empty. And I have to thank Scotty Cameron. Scotty had me on his computerized stroke analyzer for several hours the other day and we realized I was taking the putter back two degrees outside. I couldn't believe it. All along I thought I had it dead square.

ANNOUNCER: Yeah ... well ... and now back to Brandel Chamblee on 14.

Five minutes later in the locker room, Ron, whose friends all call him Ronnie, is describing his round to his pal Mike, who goes large-mouth bass fishing with him back home in Louisiana on off weeks.

"Gawdamm, Mike. That rock was diving in the hole like a homesick gopher. I musta made five three-pointers [putts outside 22 feet], and two of 'em were stone misreads. I guess if ya plumb-bob it bad enough and then pull the dogshit out of it, it's bound to go in. I'm just afraid that Doctor Karma is gonna get even with me by Sunday night."

Even if Ronnie would omit the expletives, don't you think he could endear himself more to the television audience, and make far more fans, if he let his true personality come out? I think one of the reasons the fans love John Daly so much is that he never dodges a question or gives what would be called a politically correct answer. Daly said on the Golf Channel recently that his wife was the jealous type and needed to overcome some insecurities. Now, even though that interview may have found John sleeping in the guest room that night, anyone who watched it said, "Damn, that guy's the real deal. He's Homer Simpson with spikes."

I think too many players muffle their personalities because they are trying to fit some image of the golfer as a stoic, businesslike person who keeps all his emotions inside. Granted, not everyone can be like Lee Trevino, or Fuzzy Zoeller, or Chi Chi Rodriguez, but they can be the best (fill in the name) they can be. Jay Haas doesn't exactly yuck it up on the course, but anyone who's sat with Jay for any length of time knows he's a great person with a good sense of humor. And so are most of the guys out here. You know damn well they have a lot of character and backbone. Without it, they never would have made it to golf's most demanding level. You simply cannot be a wimp and become one of the best players in the world.

So we have identified a problem. Here's a solution or two. When a tournament starts on Monday, there are a lot of opportunities for the players to get involved with the tournament proper. For the Monday pro-am, there is always a draw party Sunday night and there is always an awards party on Monday. The players are welcome at these gigs.

On Tuesday, there is a clinic, and an opportunity to visit charities or hospitals, which is a great benefit to the community and the sponsors, not to mention what it does for the spirits of a person who's having a tough time. Occasionally there is a junior clinic in the afternoon. Then on Tuesday evening, there is the draw party for the Wednesday pro-am. The Wednesday pro-am is a chance to make friends or fans that will last through the years. Why shouldn't players have lunch, or at the very least a beverage, with the amateurs when the round is completed? Sometimes an amateur contestant has a suite on the golf course, and that person, obviously a big supporter of the tournament, would more often than not be flattered if the Tour player came back to the suite for a few minutes. The Wednesday evening awards party often has high-quality entertainment like Hootie and the Blowfish, the Eagles, Huey Lewis and the News, or Sheryl Crow, so if a player has a mid-morning or later tee time, that Wednesday party is a great opportunity for him to thank the right people and show his support. The tournament organizers and sponsors always remember the players who support these activities early in the week. These events are not mandatory, but I think some of them should be.

In a tournament like Memphis, sponsored by Federal Express, the company usually reserves about three great restaurants with parties of twenty or more going to dinner throughout the week. Think how nice it would be if a player would go to the tournament director and say, "I'd be happy to go to dinner one night with the group going to Morton's." It would be worth thousands of dollars of positive PR to the corporate sponsor if the player would be willing to socialize like that and answer some basic questions about his life on Tour.

I would recommend to all players, especially the newer guys on Tour, that when they register for the tournament on Sunday or Monday or Tuesday, they stop by the tournament director's office to say hi and to let him know that if they can do something to help him make the week go smoother, or attend a function for an hour or two, they would be happy to do it. I almost never see that happening and it's a shame, and a lost opportunity to generate goodwill.

I typically hear two responses from amateurs who play in the Monday or Wednesday pro-ams on Tour. The most common is to remark about the pro's personality, and how much conversation he shared with the amateurs, and whether he helped them read putts and strategize their shots. But then there are those who critique the pro's round, and God forbid if the pro didn't play lights-out, he can get sautéed by his amateur in the 19th hole post-round breakdown.

I'll never forget playing in the pro-am preceding the B.C. Open in Endicott, New York. It was about my second full year on Tour, in 1978. I made seven birdies and eleven pars and shot 65. My wife, Jan, and I went to dinner that night with my amateur team, and we were having a great time. There was another guy at our table who had played that day and all he did was bitch about his pro and the fact that he'd made only two birdies for the team.

I said, "Well, was he pleasant to play with?"

And the guy said, "Oh, he was an awesome guy and we had fun, but he only made two birdies, the son of a bitch. He was really a lightweight when it came to helping the team."

I said, "Whoa, dude, you know some days you make a lot of putts and some days you don't."

He said, "Oh, c'mon. You guys do this for a living. You should average six birdies a day. How many did you make today?"

I said, "I happened to make seven."

And he said, "See!"

Now obviously, the fact that the professional was considerate to his partners and a pleasure to play with wasn't nearly enough to satisfy this guy. But that response is the exception, not the rule. By and large, amateurs in pro-ams just want to be treated with courtesy, engaged in light conversation, and made to feel like they're not totally out of place walking beside the pro. Damn, for $5,000 they're at least entitled to a certain level of respect and interaction. And they don't always get it. I have actually been told by a Tour player that his goal is to say as little as possible to his amateur partners. In fact, a name pro once bragged that he actually got through a round of golf without having one meaningful conversational give-and-take with any of his partners. I won't mention his name, but if he reads this, I hope it pisses him off.

AT THE SONY OPEN IN HAWAII the second event on the 2004 schedule, all the attention was rightly on Michelle Wie. There was all sorts of talk, just as there had been when Annika Sorenstam competed at Colonial the previous year, that maybe she didn't belong in the field. I feel strongly that a tournament sponsor can use his sponsors' exemptions however he sees fit, to make his tournament more competitive, or to give a local favorite a spot, or to make his event more attractive for television. The people at Sony certainly had every right to offer Michelle a spot, and boy did she prove to her naysayers that she deserved it.

Someone asked me beforehand to predict her score, and I said something like 76–76 for a total of 152—and there would have been no shame in that. Waialae Country Club had turned two par 5s into par 4s, to make it a tough par-70 course, so I wasn't belittling her to predict she would shoot that score. Damn, 152 would have been an astoundingly good score for any other fourteen-year-old girl on the planet. So she went out there and shot 72–68 for an even-par score of 140, and beat my prediction by twelve pops. Michelle birdied the last hole, and when she finished she thought she'd made the cut right on the number. As it turned out, she fell one stroke short, which was an absolutely astounding feat considering all the scrutiny and pressure she was under.

Yes, it certainly helped that she was playing in front of a home crowd, and yes, she knew the course well, but I still thought what she accomplished that week was remarkable. When you consider that the best woman player alive, Annika Sorenstam, had missed the cut by four strokes playing in a much smaller field at Colonial, and here was a young kid, missing the cut by just one in a full-field event, what can you say? Michelle made the whole week very special for anyone watching.

Let me go back for a minute to Annika's appearance in Fort Worth in May '03. I never thought she would shoot 145. I thought that was a super performance as well. The media exposure was just insane that week. Before the tournament started, I'll bet I was asked twenty times by reporters what I thought about her competing that week, and my response never varied. I said I was glad she was here, that she was very welcome, and if she wanted to use my locker she was welcome to it. I would even have showered with her, but that might not have gone over big with either of our spouses.

I feel the players who criticized her for being there just didn't know what to think. The defending champion, Nick Price, who is as nice a guy as we have on Tour, said he felt somewhat slighted by all the attention she was getting, and Vijay Singh really stuck his neck out with some of his comments. But those guys certainly had a right to their opinions. I just disagreed.

Annika deserved an A-plus for the way she handled herself the entire week. With her demeanor, she dispelled the notion that she was just an ice princess. She has never shown more personality and grace than she did at Colonial. I thought she was totally awesome and did a great service to women's golf.

And there's a story behind the story that was equally cool. The title sponsor for Colonial is Bank of America, and the director of sports marketing for B of A at that time is a friend of mine, a woman named Dockery Clark. She's been in the sports business for several years, originally working for a company called Imperial Chemical Industries. When she took over the job of sports marketing at Bank of America and the opportunity came up to have Annika play, I knew that Dockery would be all over the idea, and she was. She beat everybody to the punch. It's common sense: 50 percent of the people in the country who have banking needs are women. Having a woman in the field was appealing to them. Plus, the European market idolizes Annika for being perhaps the best woman golfer ever. She's a national hero in Sweden. The Colonial also drew more media than it ever had before or since. So the week was not only a triumph for Annika and ladies' golf, but a huge win for Bank of America and Dockery Clark. Sometimes you have to look at the global picture to appreciate these things.

For week number three on the 2004 PGA Tour schedule, we were back on the mainland at the Bob Hope Chrysler Classic. I knew it would be a nostalgic several days because it was the first "Hope" since Bob died the previous year. I had talked with the tournament director, Michael Millthorpe, several months before about bringing back a celebrity skills challenge to be held the Tuesday of tournament week. It had been done in the past and we thought it should be resurrected. I got Mark O'Meara and John Cook and Billy Andrade to participate with me, and we partnered up with George Lopez, Darius Rucker from Hootie and the Blowfish, Craig T. Nelson, and Roger Clemens and held the event at the Palmer Course at PGA West. We drew about a thousand people and had a great time, and afterward we mingled with tournament sponsors and volunteers. It's precisely the kind of activity that the Tour needs more of, because it's a way to give back to the people who make each tournament possible. I've always felt that the Hope and the Crosby, which is now called the AT&T National Pro-Am, are two of the most important tournaments on our calendar. As far as tradition and fun go, you can't beat those two events. I know a lot of pros skip them because it means playing with amateurs for three or four days and having to play different courses every day, but so what?

It frustrated me this year when Tiger said he was not going to play at the AT&T in 2004 because of the slow rounds of golf, and the fact that the courses on the Peninsula have bumpy greens and it takes him about a month to recover his confidence after putting on them. When Tiger won the AT&T on those courses in 2000, and then the U.S. Open by fifteen shots at Pebble Beach a few months later, he didn't seem to have trouble with the greens or his confidence. As good as he is with the press, I was surprised to hear Tiger make those comments because that type of thing can affect a guy's credibility.

At the Tuesday press conference I was asked why the field was dwindling in interest and participation with some of the superstars, and why there were so many complaints about slow play and bumpy greens, and I said it bothered me. I feel the players have a responsibility to our tour to give back to great events like the Hope and the AT&T, which are so popular with television audiences and have been backbone events on the PGA Tour. The AT&T, in one form or another, dates back to 1937, when Sam Snead was the first winner, and the Bob Hope has been played without interruption since 1960, when Arnold Palmer won the first of his five desert titles. Up until the last nine or ten years, those two tournaments always drew the top players.

I said at the press conference that I would ask a player, "Do you like making your four or five million dollars a year? And if so would you sacrifice one weekend to play with celebrities or the CEO of a Fortune 500 company in a six-hour round in front of adoring fans just to give back to the Tour?" If the answer to those questions was yes, I'd tell him he needed to play the AT&T or the Hope. I think that using the bumpy greens and slow play as an excuse not to play is a cop-out. If guys don't want to play, don't play. But to say you don't want to play Pebble Beach, which so many players including Jack Nicklaus rank as their favorite course in the world, just doesn't pass the truth test.

As long as I'm not getting in someone's way and I can be fairly competitive, I want to continue to play both of those tournaments because they mean a great deal to me. I was honored to know Bob and Dolores Hope, and although I did not get to know Bing Crosby very well, I kind of felt like my longtime partner Jack Lemmon became the unofficial host of that event after Bing's death, and I was so close to Jack and Clint Eastwood that I feel a responsibility to do whatever I can to help keep those events as popular as they've been through the years.

The fact that I have won both tournaments is also very special to me. I won the Hope in 1990, a couple of years after my brother Paul died after being treated at the Betty Ford Center. And I won the AT&T in 1995, shooting 17 under par in what was probably the best four-day tournament I've ever played. For me, it's kind of a testament to the fact that you can actually play good golf while having a good time with your partners and the gallery. However, I should say I've never entered either of those tournaments with a game face, or with the sole desire to win. In both cases it happened *because* I was having a good time, rather than *in spite of* enjoying myself.

I was able to continue my solid play of 2004 in the AT&T, shooting a pair of 70s and a pair of 71s. It may not sound spectacular, but in these halcyon days of great purses, my tie for fourteenth banked $95,400. For the first four weeks of the season, I shot even par or better in all seventeen rounds, which I was very pleased about. But ever since Tiger came on the scene, you have to go really deep to win tournaments. It seems like it takes a minimum of 16 or 17 under par every week to whip the field. That certainly wasn't the way it was when I came out here in 1976. A dozen under par was almost certain to be low every week, unless it was a major championship. However, we also didn't have high-tech drivers that required a full paragraph just to list the specs. Nor did we have guys doing three hundred sit-ups a day and pumping iron. It also took a little longer for rookies coming on Tour to get acclimated or get over being starstruck. Now when these young men come out of college, they've seen so much quality competition through their junior golf days and college years, and they've done so much traveling along the way, that life on the Tour isn't that big an adjustment.

When I was a junior golfer, there were only two or three tournaments a year where I could measure myself against the country's best young players. Now, with a full American Junior Golf Association schedule pitting the best against one another anywhere from ten to fifteen times a year, by the time a good junior gets to college he's pretty battle-tested.

THERE'S A STORY that says volumes about how professional golf has changed through the years. In 1991, I was playing in the Masters, and as I was about to be introduced on Thursday, I greeted the three honorary starters who were seated on the first tee. They were all golfing immortals: Gene Sarazen, Byron Nelson, and Sam Snead. At the time, I represented Toyota and so of course had my Toyota visor on, which I was contractually obligated to wear. My pairing got a nice ovation as we walked to the tee, and Mr. Sarazen, "the Squire," sort of caught me off-guard by saying, "Hey, Peter, how much did they pay you to put that car on your head?"

Now even though Mr. Sarazen was about ninety years old at the time, there was a certain edge to his comment, and I sensed he was digging me pretty good.

I politely responded with, "Ah, Mr. Sarazen, they don't pay me that much."

But he wasn't through. He said, "You kids will do anything to make money . . . all of these endorsements today."

I couldn't tell if he was scolding me or making a comment he thought the gallery might find amusing. Regardless, I took off my visor and put it on my bag. And I said, "Well, Mr. Sarazen, in honor of you I will remove the visor and tee off without a car on my head."

Everybody laughed at that, but I could tell that the Squire was still kind of irked about the fact that we were playing for all this money, or maybe it still bothered him that he had won all those major championships and earned a pittance of the prize money being offered in modern times, even if you factored in inflation. But the devil got the better of me and in a fun way I said, "Mr. Sarazen, you probably would have done the same thing I'm doing ... if they'd *had* automobiles back when you were playing."

Well, I thought Lord Byron and Slammin' Sammy were going to fall off their chairs they were laughing so hard. But the karma of the man who hit perhaps the most famous shot in the history of golf (a five-wood into the hole at Augusta National's 15th hole, for a double eagle that got him in a playoff and the eventual victory over Craig Wood in 1935) came back to burn me. I blocked my first drive about 40 yards right of my target and into a fairway bunker, and made bogey. Moral of the story: Don't mess with an icon.

There's no denying that corporate involvement and brand identification are what have made professional golf a lucrative business for so many of us. For decades, golf tournaments happened because they were organized by well-intentioned individuals in a community that loved golf, wanted to see the best players, and hoped to raise some dollars for their favorite local charities. Sometimes they'd raise $50,000 or maybe even $100,000, and everyone was happy. But in the 1950s and early sixties there were only about ten to fifteen players making a good living in the game. Jackie Burke told me that even though he won the PGA and the Masters in 1956, he didn't play in the U.S. Open that year because he had to return to his club professional job at Winged Foot. Can you imagine a player today who is talented enough to win two majors in the same season skipping the other majors because he has to go to work? The idea is preposterous.

However, once Arnold Palmer started capturing the country's attention around 1960 and turning televised golf tournaments into a strong draw, corporations realized they could identify and brand their product with a good clean sport that businesspeople and consumers enjoyed playing. That's why we no longer play the Doral Open, but rather the Ford Championship at Doral, and the L.A.

Open is now the Nissan Open, and the Bing Crosby is the AT&T National Pro-Am. Not only could a company more clearly elevate the image of its product, but it could entertain customers and clients with corporate hospitality functions throughout the week.

Corporate hospitality is now the heart and soul of the economics of the PGA Tour. Phoenix has what they call the "Bird's Nest," which hosts kick-ass parties during the FBR Open. It used to be an on-site gathering, but now it's held off-site with adult beverages and rock 'n' roll bands, and it becomes almost an after-hours ticket to the tournament. It's through corporate sponsorship and dramatically increased television ratings for golf over the last decade that we have seen the purses rise so dramatically. Thirty years ago, there were just sixty guys on the annual money list who were fully exempt for all tournaments the following year, and in 1973, the sixtieth money earner won about $55,000. That means he was doing slightly better than breaking even. In 2004, there were 125 men on the money list who remained fully exempt, and the player at number 125, Tag Ridings, won $623,262. If you won $55,000 in 2004, you might be spending the next year on the Hooters Tour, eating chicken wings at Hooters, but only on two-for-one night and only if your wife was in another city.

Some of the credit also goes to the manufacturers of golf equipment, who have improved the technology of the clubs and balls to the point where average golfers are constantly upgrading their equipment. The typical 12-handicapper has to have the latest innovation that gives him 10 extra yards or takes some of the snap out of his snap-hooked tee shots. If the weekend golfer has the "Swinging Dick" driver and he hears that Ernie Els has suddenly switched to the "Big Swinging Dick" driver, then he's got to have it to keep his edge over the other boys in the weekend choose-'em-up game.

Certainly the players on the professional tours deserve much of the credit as well. The talent level has gotten so much deeper, it's incredible. Not long ago Jack Nicklaus alluded to the fact that in his heyday there were fewer really top-notch players. Nicklaus said he had only a handful of players he felt he had to beat to win a golf tournament, and thus his era created more great players with sterling résumés because they were able to pile up more victories and more major championships. In this day and age, anyone who wins three majors is considered an absolute superstar. Nick Price got in the World Golf Hall of Fame two years ago at age forty-six, and Greg Norman at the same age. Price has three majors and Norman two. Are they deserving? Absolutely. But two majors back in the day wouldn't have earned entry into the Hall of Fame.

When I first started on Tour, even par would nearly always make the thirty-six-hole cut, and sometimes 2 or 3 over was good enough. Nowadays, courses are set up to be more difficult and are much longer (to compensate for technological advances in balls and clubs), and the Tour staff is setting the pins in far tougher spots. Sometimes, standing in the middle of the fairway 180 yards from the green, you'd swear the flagstick isn't even on the green. As one caddie graphically put it, "I can tend the flagstick and take a piss in the rough at the same time." And still, even with all those added challenges, it usually takes 2 or 3 under par just to play the weekend.

The fitness level of players is uniformly high, and the average player is taller and stronger than in past years. The top five players in the world, as I'm writing this, are all at least six feet tall, whereas thirty or forty years ago a player who was six feet tall was an anomaly. All the greats of the 1950s were from five-seven to five-eleven: Hogan, Palmer, Player, Nicklaus, then Trevino, and later Watson. These were the men who won major championships by the bushel in the quarter century before this quarter century, and if they played basketball in high school I assure you they were point guards.

WHO CAN FORGET the 2004 Masters when Arnold made his fiftieth and final playing appearance at Augusta National? As he walked up the 18th fairway on Friday to an enormous ovation, the announcers showed their respect by going dead silent (when was the last time you heard *that*?). I think all true golfers in the country had tears in their eyes. And when Arnie was interviewed in Butler Cabin after the round, and he was so choked up he could barely speak, I noticed that none of his comments were about his own performance out there. Arnold has known and accepted for a long time that golf is a hard game. He didn't say, "I was disappointed in the way I drove the ball," or "My putting was substandard." His entire thought process was to thank the fans and to thank the members of Augusta National for the opportunity to play the course for fifty years and for giving him a career in golf.

Perhaps no player in the history of modern professional golf has connected with fans like Arnie, and no player of his era ever spent more time functioning as the conscience of the game and educating younger players on the right way to act as a professional golfer.

I used to play every year in a one-day exhibition to benefit a children's hospital at Annandale Country Club in California. It would be Arnie and me joined by Pat Rielly, who was then president of the PGA of America, and a top lady professional like Jan Stephenson or Juli Inkster. This was in the late 1980s. The day consisted of a breakfast, a clinic, a round of golf, and cocktails afterward. During one round, as we were walking from a green to the next tee and I was signing an autograph, Arnold suddenly shoved a hat in my face and said, "What the hell is that?"

I said, "Uh, that's my autograph."

Palmer said, "Well, I can't read it, and if *I* can't read it, these people can't read it. Why in the hell would they want your name on a hat if they get home and can't read it? Sign the damn thing so they can read it."

He said it so emphatically I knew he wasn't kidding around. Since that moment, I've tried to sign my autograph as legibly as I can.

Here's where something has been lost in translation. Nowadays when I am handed a hat to sign, I see sometimes ten or fifteen signatures on it and I can't read a single one of them. An autograph looks like the guy put his pen to the hat while he was ice skating and then slipped and fell in a hole in the ice as he was signing. The scrawl marks go everywhere. Or it's like the player was writing his name in English using the Arabic alphabet. That scribble might work on a personal check, but not on a souvenir hat. I've talked to guys about taking a little more care when they sign, but apparently I haven't imparted the message as effectively as Arnold did with me, because the signatures these days are pathetic.

A few years ago, I had an "Arnie moment" like that with a young player whom I happen to like a lot, Jonathan Kaye. This young man's got a ton of talent and I believe he'll win a lot of golf tournaments before he's through, possibly a major. Anyway, this occurred at the B.C. Open, probably in Jonathan's first or second year on Tour. I was playing with Chip Beck, we were on the 13th tee, and across the pond was Kaye, putting on the 1st hole, which was his tenth of the day. He had a 6-footer for birdie, and he missed the putt—apparently the ball hit a mark on the green and popped up—and he wasn't happy. He angrily whacked the green and took a divot out of it. You could have planted corn in the scar. Then he barely tapped down the damage and stormed off the green.

I was shocked and could barely believe what I'd seen. So I yelled across, "Jonathan, Jonathan!"

He just kept on walking like he hadn't heard me. I chased him down and said, "Are you the last pairing out here today?"

"No," he said.

"Well then, somebody behind you is going to have to putt over that mark you left. Now go back and fix it." And I made him go back and repair the dent in the green.

I know Jonathan hated my guts for that, and he consciously avoided me for about a month afterward. He probably thought I was a prick in capital letters, but the part of him that understands the game knew clearly after the fact that I was right, and he was clearly in the wrong. I know damn well he'd have been hot if he'd had to putt over that thing after someone else had gone ballistic. Today we laugh about it, but he's never forgotten the moment. If you ever walk up to Jonathan and ask him about Peter Jacobsen and the B.C. Open, he'd cringe at the memory. But those are the kinds of things that veteran players have to do to pass the baton.

And this is what has given the Tour such a classy reputation. I can't think of anything else I'd rather do or anywhere else I'd rather be. Playing with these guys has been the thrill of my life for nearly thirty years now, and if some of the players I've been writing about in this book are any guide, I expect to be here for a good many years yet.

I hope you enjoyed reading *Embedded Balls* as much as Jack and I enjoyed writing it. It only took me twelve years since *Buried Lies*—so stay tuned for 2017. I'll grab my walker and we'll go another round!

ACKNOWLEDGMENTS

No PROFESSIONAL GOLFER functions in a void. We are only as effective as the great people who support us. Many thanks to the following for all they've done for me: Mike Cowan, Dave Pelz, Stan Utley, Jim Hardy, Chuck Hogan, Randy and Ross Henry, Dr. Richard Coop, Jennifer Munro, Ed Ellis, Alana Snyder, Pam Armstrong, the staff at PJP, Chris and Mike O'Connell, Rick Sellers, Matt Griesser, Terry Trebelhorn, Jay Kossoff, and Justine Zilliken.